Liverpool *to* **Loggerheads**

A celebration of the close links
between **Merseyside** and
North Wales

Lorna Jenner

Copyright © 2009 **Alyn Books** Ltd, The Nook, Pentre Road, Cilcain, Mold, Flintshire CH7 5PD.

ISBN 978-0-9559625-2-3

Editing: Sarah Brennen

Design and mapping: William Smuts

Printed by: Gomer Press, Llandysul, Ceredigion

With special thanks to:

All the people from North Wales and Merseyside who have taken the time to tell me their touching and heart-warming stories. Space has limited what could be included and I apologise to those whose stories are not recounted here but all helped to set the scene and give me the flavour of events.

Liverpool Record Office

Pat Gore

The Rev D Ben Rees

Jill Wallis

Rita and Jim Sharp

Sue and Ian Morris

Alec Butler

Vic Mason, Maidie Brown and Jackie Robertson

Dedicated to: My mother, May, and godmother, Betty, whose memories first inspired me to write this book.

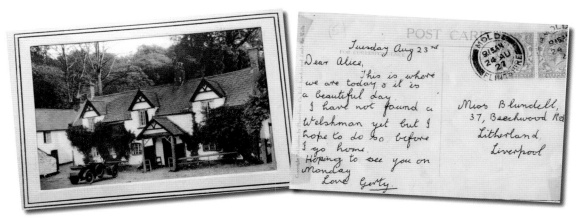

Postcard sent from Loggerheads, 1927
Courtesy of Colomendy Museum

Grant-aided by the AONB Sustainable Development Fund

Foreword

The Clwydian Range is a special area to many people. The heather clad hills, the steep wooded valleys and the dramatic rocky outcrops are all part of the natural beauty that makes it so special. Beauty, however, is more than just skin deep and it is the people that give an area its personality and its unique character.

Generations of communities have shaped the land, farming, building and moulding the landscape to meet their needs. It is people that give an area its flavour, its culture and its heritage, accumulated over many generations. Around Moel Famau and Loggerheads, an important part of this culture comes from Merseyside. Just as the Welsh have contributed to the rich mix of Liverpudlian culture over the years, in this area, the Liverpudlian input has been considerable.

For generations the people of Merseyside have come to North Wales to live, to work, and to relax and unwind. Merseyside children took refuge here during the war years and later families and youngsters came to escape the city and to enjoy the open air. Generations of school children came to Colomendy, 'the lung of Liverpool', others came by bike or with the Scouts and Guides, on the Crosville buses, or with their tents and caravans. Over time the people of Merseyside have formed a bond with the Loggerheads area and have a special relationship with it. Some have stayed and have become locals themselves.

You do not have to dig too deeply to find links to Merseyside in most local families. A link is rarely more than one or two generations away, if not a direct family tie, a connection, perhaps evacuees coming to stay or family members seeking work across the water. All these individual stories combine to add a cultural layer to the landscape and give a unique flavour to the area.

This book tells some of those stories and in doing so celebrates the bond between Merseyside and the Clwydian Range. It is based on many fascinating, often moving, conversations and on memories that have been shared willingly and fondly.

The Clwydian Range was designated an Area of Outstanding Natural Beauty in 1985, in recognition of the nationally important quality of its landscape. The interaction of the people of Merseyside with people of North Wales has contributed to its special quality, helping to define it and shape its unique local character.

David Shiel, Countryside Officer, Clwydian Range
Area of Outstanding Natural Beauty, May 2009

AHNE Bryniau Clwyd
Clwydian Range AONB

Contents

City of Liverpool
RHIWLAS STREET L8

Why are there such close ties?

Chapter 1

Two octagenarian Liverpudlian cousins (my mother and my godmother) met a couple of years ago in Cornwall. Neither had lived in Liverpool for many years and hadn't seen each other for a while. As we sat down with a glass of red wine, one turned to the other and said, 'Iechyd da, cariad bach!' (Good health, my little darling!) It was touching to hear these Liverpudlian ladies as they later reminisced about their Welsh heritage. Neither have more than a smattering of the language but are both proud of their Welsh ancestry. I started to listen more actively and ask questions when they talked about their past.

When I moved to North East Wales myself 10 years ago I noticed the scouse twang of many of the voices, and have been surprised by how many of the local people had roots in Merseyside. Whilst conducting visitor surveys at Loggerheads Country Park, Merseyside visitors dominated, often 2 or 3 generations of the same family, brought back by enthusiastic grandparents who had such fond memories of the area. I knew that the Country Park had originally been founded by Crosville Motor Services bringing day trippers from Merseyside and also knew that Colomendy Environmental Centre nearby was owned by Liverpool Education Authority but realised gradually that the relationship between Merseyside and North Wales was much deeper than I had at first thought. This book aims to explore and celebrate this strong relationship.

The Liverpool Welsh

To begin to understand why the interrelationship between the 2 areas is so strong, one must first look back in history to the late 18th century when the port of Liverpool began to grow. The city continued to expand throughout the 19th century, as the port became one of the largest in Europe and the gateway to America, bringing wealth and prosperity to the city.

Thousands of enterprising young Welsh men and women flocked to Liverpool from rural North Wales, drawn by the chance of jobs and, for the entrepreneurs, exciting business opportunities. Others arrived in Liverpool intending to emigrate but some of these decided to stay, drawn by the opportunities that the developing city offered. The Liverpool Welsh, as they were known, became an integral part of the Liverpool scene. Welsh immigration remained steady throughout the 19th and the early 20th centuries so there was always a fresh stream of arrivals, keeping the language and culture alive in the metropolis. Whilst the Irish connections with the city are well-known, the story of the Welsh in Liverpool has

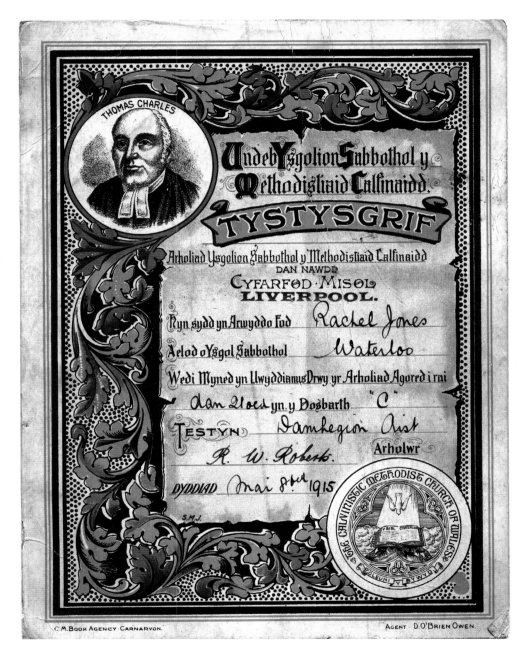

THOMAS CHARLES

Undeb Ysgolion Sabbothol y Methodistiaid Calfinaidd.

TYSTYSGRIF

Arholiad Ysgolion Sabbothol y Methodistiaid Calfinaidd
DAN NAWDD
CYFARFOD MISOL
LIVERPOOL.

Hyn sydd yn Arwyddo Fod   Rachel Jones

Aelod o Ysgol Sabbothol   Waterloo

Wedi Myned yn Llwyddianus Drwy yr Arholiad Agored i rai

Dan 21 oed yn y Dosbarth   "C"

TESTYN   Damhegion Crist

R. W. Roberts   Arholwr

DYDDIAD   Mai 8fed 1915

S.M.J.

C.M. BOOK AGENCY CARNARVON.   AGENT D.O'BRIEN OWEN.

Welsh Sunday school certificate from Waterloo Chapel, Liverpool

Courtesy of Mair Lloyd

sometimes been overlooked although their influence was considerable. Many of the young men, who arrived in Liverpool with very little money, became, within 30 years, affluent and successful builders and merchants who had a significant impact on Liverpool society and commerce. Even the name of the city is thought to have come from the Welsh 'Lle'r pwll', meaning 'the place of the pool'. Welsh surnames like Morris, Williams, Griffiths and Jones are still common in Liverpool, showing that many families have distant Welsh forebears, although they may not sound Welsh today.

There was a great demand for servants for the grand houses being built by the prospering middle classes - bankers, brokers, merchants - and many thousands of young Welsh women went into service in Liverpool.

Ffion Hughes' great grandmother, Nain Ffon, went to work in Liverpool, looking after the children of a chapel minister. She stayed in the city during the week but commuted home at weekends on the Liverpool - Llandudno ferry.

Men had a much wider choice of work. The port itself offered plenty of work opportunities. Many experienced seamen from along the North Wales coast moved to Liverpool to take up work on the larger ships that were registered

St Tudno SS brought workers to Liverpool from along the Welsh coast

Courtesy of Liverpool Record Office, Liverpool Libraries

there. Others worked as boiler makers and fitters at the boat-building yards, as dockers loading and unloading the cargoes or as clerks at the shipping and associated finance houses.

The experience of the Williams family was typical. **May D'Arcy (neé Williams)** *recalls: "The Williams were a shipping family from Holyhead with all 5 brothers employed in ship-related work. My father, a merchant seaman, and one of his younger brothers, a boiler maker, eventually moved to Liverpool as there were better job prospects in the bigger port. First one brother married a Liverpool girl and later his brother married her younger sister!"*

The largest area of male employment was in the building trade and the Liverpool Welsh played a key role in the building of both the docks and the expanding city. Many people associate large-scale building with the Irish - the Irish 'navvie' or labourer is a familiar phrase - and Liverpool undoubtedly had large numbers of Irish immigrants. However, it was the Welsh who dominated the Liverpool building trade. Welsh chapel minister and acclaimed historian, Ben Rees estimates that two thirds of the city was built by the Welsh and, by the late 19th century, most of the construction in Liverpool was in Welsh hands. Some established large building companies and became very wealthy, forming a Welsh bourgeoisie or middle class.

Mair Lloyd was born in Llanarmon-yn-Iâl but her family have strong links with Liverpool. "My great uncle, Huw Roberts, moved from Dolgellau to Liverpool to work as a builder. He established a successful building company in Orrell Park, which still operates today. My mother was brought up in Liverpool with her uncle's family and attended the Welsh chapel in Waterloo but later returned to Wales and ran the village Post Office in Llanarmon. My father's mother also worked in Liverpool and, when she returned to Llanarmon, she renamed the village shop, 'Liverpool House', in recognition of the family links to the city!"

The movement between Liverpool and North Wales was two-way.

David Sibeon recalls: "My great great grandfather Isaac Sibeon moved from a lead miner's cottage near Holywell, to Pall Mall in Liverpool in the 1820s and worked as a plasterer. My great grandfather returned to Holywell, after his mother died of typhoid, and established a thriving building firm that built many of the civic buildings in Holywell around the end of the 19th century."

It was not only the workforce that came from Wales, but also much of the building material. Bricks from Ruabon were used to build Liverpool University in 1892, giving rise to the term, 'red-brick universities'; Welsh slates roofed many of the buildings and vast amounts of limestone from North Wales were imported for building programmes. Hydraulic lime that would set under water came from Halkyn Mountain in Flintshire and was used to build Birkenhead Docks. More recently, in the 1960s, limestone aggregate from a Halkyn quarry was used to build one of Liverpool's most familiar landmarks, the Metropolitan Cathedral, and Welsh stone has continued to be in demand.

Ifor Thomas lives in Gwernymynydd but his family have a long association with Liverpool and the construction industry as his taid and his brother lived in the city when they were working on the digging of the Mersey Railway Tunnel in the 1880s. Ifor himself worked at limestone quarries in the 1960s and 70s. He recalls, "I drove a lorry taking quarried stone to customers and many of my trips were to Merseyside. I particularly remember delivering stone for the building of Seaforth Docks as a massive amount was needed and the lorries were working day and night. I also delivered stone for the extension to Alder Hey Children's Hospital and took numerous loads of tarmac for road surfacing across Merseyside."

Other notable Welsh successes were in the retail trade. Owen Owen from Penmaenmawr initially opened up a small drapery shop on London Road then, as it expanded, moved to a large department store on Clayton Square. TJ Hughes, founded in 1912, followed later.

"A lot of Welsh people used to shop at Owen Owen on a Thursday. They sold

things like crockery, furniture and clothes. There was a little shop downstairs where you could buy speciality foods."

Lewis's was opened in 1856 as a men's clothing store by Welshman, David Lewis, mostly manufacturing his own stock. In 1864, Lewis's branched out into women's clothing. In the 1870s, the store expanded and added new departments, including shoes in 1874 and tobacco in 1879.

Many also came to Liverpool to train in medical science or nursing as Cardiff, the only Welsh medical school, was inaccessible to students from North Wales as the journey was so long and difficult.

Gordon (Gwilym) Short came from Bangor to train as a pharmacist in 1939. "At first I struggled to converse in English. Chapel was a great comfort as I could relax there and speak in my native tongue. When I set up my own pharmacy I anglicised my Christian name as the locals found Gordon far easier to say than Gwilym!"

Welsh street names in Toxteth

Welsh Liverpool

The Welsh settled in 3 main areas: to the north-east in the suburbs of Everton, some streets in central Liverpool and southern suburban areas around Toxteth Park, whose Victorian terraces have typical Welsh names like Kinmel, Rhiwlas and Voelas. Over the years the more affluent Welsh speaking community moved from the 'close-knit' inner city areas to more affluent areas like Penny Lane and Allerton. In the 19th century, the city-centre's Pall Mall was known as 'Little Wales' and it was the site of the first Welsh Chapel in Liverpool.

In 1813, one in every 10 people in Liverpool was Welsh and a high percentage could only speak their native tongue. In the 1870s, a further 50,000 Welsh people moved to the city, making it the unofficial 'Capital of North Wales'. In the early 20th century it had a larger Welsh speaking presence than Cardiff or Swansea, Wrexham or Newport!

Many large and imposing Welsh chapels and churches, were built to serve the flourishing community, including some of the largest Welsh nonconformist chapels anywhere in the United Kingdom. Toxteth Chapel was for a long time the largest Welsh Chapel in the world and some of the chapels attracted the largest congregations in the history of Welsh Calvinistic Methodism – in Wales, England or America!

Chapel was the hub of life for most of the Liverpool Welsh, providing far more than a place of worship. It was usually the first port of call for newly arriving Welsh folk and they were key meeting places. Many found jobs through the chapels, taken on by Welsh building firms and shop owners, whose wealthy owners were often elders in the chapels, or going into service with the Welsh middle classes. The chapels provided a social life for many of the new arrivals, many of whom spoke very little English. For these young folk, going to Welsh chapel helped to stem their homesickness, giving them something familiar and a link to their Welsh roots. The chapels even served as dating agencies for the young Welsh as many married within the Liverpool Welsh community!

*The Welsh community in Bootle was still thriving when **Olive Short (neé Lewis)** grew up there in the 1930s, having moved to the city when she was 5. Olive recalls: "I attended chapel and competed in Cymanfa Ganu, (singing competitions), like any child growing up in my native Anglesey would have done."*

Other Liverpool Welsh integrated and married outside the Welsh community. Sometimes there was a clash of

cultures when Welsh and Liverpudlians intermarried.

Ffion Hughes remembers stories of her great nain's disapproval of her sister's choice of husband. Her family were devout chapel-goers and were teetotal, whereas her sister's Liverpudlian husband enjoyed a few drinks - the marriage didn't last!

Many intermarriages were much more successful but the Welsh incomers still found ways to retain their Welshness.

May D'Arcy had a Welsh father and Liverpudlian mother. "My father and his brother did not speak Welsh at home with their Liverpudlian families but they enjoyed going to the Welsh chapel in Bootle together, as much to speak and sing in Welsh as to worship. I have lasting memories of listening to my father and his 2 brothers gathered round the parlour fire on Boxing Day singing Calon Lân and other Welsh songs, each taking a different part and harmonising."

Music, literature and poetry are at the core of the Welsh culture, and, within the city, bards, scholars and hymnists came from the ranks of the Liverpool Welsh. The National Eisteddfod was staged in Liverpool 5 times between 1884 and 1929. The best known Merseyside Eisteddfod is perhaps the Birkenhead Eisteddfod of 1917 when the Eisteddfod Chair was draped in black as it was awarded posthumously to the renowned poet Hedd Wyn who had been killed in action in World War One. The Liverpool Welsh Choral Union, founded for the 1900 Liverpool Eisteddfod, is still active today. Liverpool was one of the centres for publishing Welsh language books and newspapers, some with a circulation across Wales. A local Welsh language paper, Yr Angor, still exists today.

The visual link

Geographical proximity is one obvious reason for the close relationship. However, many other equally beautiful landscapes lie within easy reach of Liverpool, including the South Pennines, the Trough of Bowland and Southern Lakeland, so what is the special pull of North Wales? The strong visual link plays an important part. The North Wales coast is clearly visible across the water and the iconic shape of Moel Famau, crowned by the castle-like ruins of the Jubilee Tower, can be seen from many parts of Liverpool and the Wirral. Conversely, the Liverpool skyline is visible from Moel Famau and the North Wales coast on a clear day. Many people have mentioned their early memories of looking across at the Clwydian skyline.

Nancy Willan, who spent many years in Cilcain, at the foot of Moel Famau, as an evacuee and on holiday, commented: "Moel Famau has been a thread, albeit a slender one, running through my life. When I was tiny my mother used to take me in my pushchair to Penny Lane railway bridge from where we had a good view of the Clwydian Range. I suppose I became a little possessive of it – after all it played a big part in my life."

Colin Legg, who was born in Liverpool but now lives in Rhes-y-cae, recalls: "Moel Famau was always familiar to me, even as a young child in Liverpool. I saw it each day as I walked over Mossley Hill to Sudley Road Primary School. Now I'm retired I see Moel Famau every day from my cottage at Rhes-y-cae."

Former Colomendy pupil, the late Doug Stephenson, wrote, "I spent my early years in Aigburth, always within site of the Mersey and the Clwydian Mountain Range beyond. So many Liverpool children must have been brought up in the same environment, looking at those same mysterious hills....."

The capital of North Wales?

By the end of the 19th century Liverpool was undoubtedly the economic capital of North Wales, the focal point for trade and commerce.

In 2003, former Clwyd West MP, Gareth Thomas, who was brought up on Merseyside, argued that it still retains its importance today, saying "North Wales still looks to Liverpool as the capital to this day. The ties of affinity are far greater between North Wales and Liverpool than between North Wales and Cardiff."

The topography of Wales with its mountainous central region has always made the journey to Cardiff difficult and, even today, there is no direct route by road or train. Liverpool, however, is far closer and the transport links, first by boat and later by train and road, have always been good.

It is no coincidence that Merseyside and North Wales were originally one region in both the Youth Hostel Association and the Ramblers Association. This reflected the large numbers of Merseysiders who used North Wales as their playground to cycle, walk and camp. Whilst they now form separate regions within both organisations, North Wales remains a popular holiday and day out destination for Merseysiders, bringing significant economic benefits to North Wales.

The traffic is still two-way. In recent times, footballers Ian Rush and Michael Owen are probably some of Flintshire's best known exports to Liverpool and there is a strong tradition of support for Liverpool Football Club in North East Wales. Many people commute daily to work in the city as Liverpool is now less than an hour's drive away from Loggerheads. Many more visit regularly to enjoy its top quality theatres, concert halls, museums and wealth of shops. The Liverpool universities remain very popular with students from North Wales. The importance of the Liverpool Welsh has decreased but the strong cultural and economic links they established between North Wales and Merseyside is their lasting legacy to both areas.

Reference: R. Merfyn Jones and D. Ben Rees; Liverpool Welsh and Their Religion; Modern Welsh Publications Ltd, 1984

View across the water from Otterspool

Courtesy of Jim Sharp

*Day trips
by boat, train,
bus and bike*

Chapter 2

N orth Wales has been a favoured place for a day out from Liverpool since Victorian times, with day trippers coming by boat, train, bus, bicycle and, more recently, by motorcar.

By Boat

From the late 19th century, paddle steamers ran regular services from Liverpool along the North Wales coast to the Menai Straits. A cruise along the Welsh coast or to one of the numerous resorts that were springing up became a popular outing. The Liverpool and North Wales Steamship Company continued to run until 1962 but passenger numbers declined steadily as car ownership increased.

The paddle steamers such as La Marguerite and the St Tudno, sailed daily in the summer season from Liverpool to Menai Bridge via Llandudno, Beaumaris and Bangor. They left Princes Landing Stage, Liverpool, at 11am returning by 7.30pm. There were also special summer excursions to Llandudno and other resorts giving a few hours ashore.

Postcard sent from the St Tudno, 1903

Courtesy of Liverpool Record Office, Liverpool Libraries

Left: On deck en route to Llandudno

Right: Relaxing on the Great Orme

Courtesy of Pat Gore

Pat Gore, *from Crosby, remembers her mother describing the excursions she used to take on the paddle steamers: "My mother and her elder sister Rose sometimes took trips on the St Seiriol or the St Tudno to Llandudno where they used to climb up the Great Orme."*

There have been ferries transporting passengers and freight across the Mersey for centuries but it was not until the early 19th century that a regular passenger paddle steamer service started. The services grew, with ferries running from Pier Head in Liverpool to Woodside in Birkenhead, Egremont, Eastham, Seacombe and New Brighton. Initially they were run by private companies but later by the Birkenhead Commissioners and the Wallasey Local Board. The record for the greatest number of passengers in any one day at Woodside was on Whit Monday 1918 when 92,789 used the ferry!

The ferries were used primarily to commute into the city but, at weekends, they became the starting point for a day trip to the Wirral and, for many, on to Wales. Passengers thronged the landing stage at Pier Head to take the ferry to Woodside then picked up a Crosville bus to Pantymwyn or Loggerheads.

The ferries were very popular with cyclists too, with hundreds taking tandems and bicycles over on the ferries to Woodside, Rock Ferry or Seacombe and then

Royal Daffodil ferry

Courtesy of Mersey Ferries, Photographer Stewart Rayner

riding into Wales. In fact, the sheer volume of cyclists at weekends caused congestion, particularly at embarkation and disembarkation. At weekends in the 1930s there were sometimes over 1,000 cyclists using the Rock Ferry service on a single trip! There was serious overcrowding on the Liverpool landing stage, with reports of cyclists jostling foot passengers. Cyclists were requested to stand back when pedestrians were disembarking but there were occasional incidents when people lost patience and tempers became frayed!

> **Frank Kennedy** *from Aigburth Vale used to cycle over on a delivery bike in the 1940s. "The Pier Head used to be chock-a-block with bikes waiting to get on the ferry to go to Wales."*

After the Mersey Railway Tunnel opened in 1886, it did take some trade from the ferries but they still remained popular. By 1894, trains were carrying 25,000 passengers per day and the ferries 44,000 per day. However, after the first of the road tunnels opened in 1934, the ferry services suffered greatly. As profits decreased, Birkenhead Corporation closed its southern terminals; New Ferry in September 1927, Eastham in 1929 and Rock Ferry in June 1939.

In 1950, the ferries were still carrying almost 30 million passengers per year but, as car ownership increased in the 1960s, passenger numbers continued to decline and had fallen to 7 million by 1970.

Investment into the Merseyrail "Liverpool Loop" extension and the opening of the 2nd road tunnel in 1971 resulted in a further decline in passenger numbers and the future of the ferry service was uncertain. Fortunately, the ferry held great sentimental value for generations of Merseysiders and there was widespread public protest when the service was threatened with closure. As a result the ferry boats were retained but the frequency of the service was reduced. Nowadays they are still popular with visitors for Mersey cruises but are no longer used as a regular commuting route to and from Liverpool or as a valued escape route into the North Wales countryside.

By train

By the late 19th century, Chester had become the hub for trains to North Wales, as it had an excellent service to Birkenhead and Liverpool and connections along the North Wales Coast and to Llangollen, Corwen and Ruthin. The opening of the Mold - Denbigh line in 1869 widened the options further, giving a train link to the Loggerheads area, via the station at Rhydymwyn. The journey was still slow - in 1903 the 29 mile journey from Chester to Denbigh took 73 minutes - but it was a popular route for holiday-makers and day trippers.

Ramblers at Rhydymwyn Station

Courtesy of W.A. Camwell

Rhydymwyn was a popular destination as it was the gateway to the beautiful Alyn Valley and connected to Loggerheads via the Leete Path. It was a great attraction for walkers and, for several years after the war, Merseyside Ramblers Association put on a 7 coach excursion train on the Mold - Denbigh line on Easter Monday, dropping walkers off at various points. Largely as a result of the railway, facilities for the visitors developed gradually, including informal campsites, cafes and other overnight accommodation.

Advert from Liverpool District Association of the Cyclists' Touring Club magazine

Following the same pattern as the ferries, widespread car ownership in the 1960s brought about the demise of the Mold – Denbigh railway and finally it closed for passengers in 1964. For almost a century it had played an important part in bringing generations of Merseysiders to the Welsh countryside.

Nant Alyn, Rhydymwyn

Courtesy of the Morris family

By Bus

Perhaps the best-known transport from Merseyside to the Loggerheads area in the mid 20th century was the Crosville bus. In the 1920s the brothers, Claude and Jim Crosland Taylor, who founded Crosville Motor Services, began running services from Birkenhead to Loggerheads and Pantymwyn, bringing day trippers and holiday-makers. From Pantymwyn, visitors would walk along the Leete Path to Loggerheads or Rhydymwyn.

Betty Earps remembers: "Early in the morning my Mum, my big sister Olwyn, our two elder brothers, Owen and Frank, and I set off from our house on Bedford Road, Liverpool. Sometimes one of our cousins came with us too so my Mum really had her hands full! First we got the tramcar to Pier Head then took the underground train to Birkenhead. Here we waited patiently to board the green Crosville Bus for the long journey to Loggerheads. Mum used to tell me to curl up tiny on her knee so that she wouldn't have to pay for me! I loved that journey as we left the city behind and the green fields and hills unfolded before us. We always got excited when we could see Moel Famau."

Early services may have used open-topped charabancs, and these continued to be chartered by groups for special outings.

Barbara Sisson lived in a two-storey block of flats in Wallasey after the war. "The residents used to run a tontine - a sort of savings club - to fund special outings. Occasionally they would use the money to hire a charabanc and everyone would have a day out in North Wales, either to Loggerheads, Prestatyn or Llandudno. The journeys seemed to take forever as I was only 5 or 6 and didn't often travel! Us children thought the outings were wonderful and I have happy memories of those visits."

A Crosville bus

Courtesy of Lorna Jenner

Loggerheads Tea Gardens

The bus trips to the We Three Loggerheads Inn proved very popular so, when the Loggerheads estate came up for auction in 1926, Claude and Jim Crosland Taylor bid to buy the inn itself. However, the price went too high so they purchased 74 acres of the land across the road instead and set up the rival Crosville Tea Garden. They built a tea-house that could accommodate parties of 100 or more and developed the tea-gardens including a band stand, putting-green, wooden swing-boats, slot machines and other attractions. The adjoining woods were also opened to the public and people enjoyed walking along the river and climbing up the steep Cat Walk to the top of the rocks. During the summer, bands and other free entertainments were laid on. The development was extremely successful with hundreds of visitors coming each weekend. Buses ran every half-hour during the summer and hourly in the winter. On summer evenings buses ran until late and large crowds gathered to catch the last buses back to Birkenhead. If there were too many passengers for one bus, Crosville put on more buses and kept running the service until the last passengers had been brought back to Birkenhead!

Crosville charabancs outside the We Three Loggerheads Inn

Courtesy of Denbighshire Countryside Service

Betty Earps remembers visiting Loggerheads in the 1930s: *"We all loved going to the tea-gardens where we played in the river and climbed up to the crags. There were swing-boats on there then and they were my favourite. I remember being told off for swinging too high!"*

Many who visited as children in the 1950s remember with fondness the arcade machines in the park.

Gordon Jones recalls visiting whilst staying at nearby Colomendy: *"During our free time we were allowed to go down to Loggerheads to the café and shop and to play on the arcade machines in the little park. A favourite was the electric shock machine. Such fun we had, paying a penny, to receive an electric shock!"*

The owner of the land adjacent to the tea-gardens developed additional visitor facilities on his land, providing parking for cars, a kiosk selling soft drinks, sweets and ice-cream, and digging a small boating lake.

Crosville Tea House

Courtesy of Denbighshire
Countryside Service

Courtesy of Denbighshire Countryside Service

Courtesy of Colomendy Museum

Courtesy of Derek Parsons

Loggerheads scenes

Courtesy of Denbighshire Countryside Service

Courtesy of May D'Arcy

Courtesy of Betty Earps

Courtesy of Denbighshire Countryside Service

*From the age of 11, **Howard Roberts** spent most of his weekends working on the car park or the boating lake and continued working there for 30 years until the 1980s. He recalls: "There were 5 motor boats on the lake that were all painted different colours. We hired them out for 10 minutes a time and they were really popular. I loved doing the work and I learned a lot about running a business, customer care and dealing with people – no one wants their car parked by a cheeky lad and politeness often earned a nice tip!"*

***Richard Davies'** grandfather was the miller at Loggerheads. He recalls: "We lived at Sawmill Cottage beside the tea-gardens and my grandmother and mother served refreshments at the cottage – pots of tea with home-made cakes, sandwiches, and boiled eggs from our own hens."*

In 1974, Crosville sold the land at Loggerheads to Clwyd County Council and it became Loggerheads Country Park (now owned by Denbighshire County Council and managed by Denbighshire Countryside Service). In 1984 the old wooden tea-house burned down and was rebuilt in stone, along with a Countryside Centre. The Country Park is now managed for wildlife as well as recreation and remains incredibly popular with visitors.

Sawmill Cottage

Courtesy of Denbighshire Countryside Service

The Bwlch from the Old Ruthin Road at Ty-Fy-Nain Moel Fammau.

The old road up Moel Famau

Courtesy of Rene Smith

Many day trippers walked from Loggerheads up Moel Famau.

*As a child **Glenys Roberts** lived in a cottage on the lane leading up to Moel Famau. "During the summer my mother used to run a café in a little room in the garden, serving teas to hikers. I used to help carrying the teas up the steps."*

From Loggerheads to Liverpool

The flow of visitors wasn't all one way. Welsh youngsters loved the excitement of an occasional trip to Liverpool to shop in the department stores, visit relatives and friends or dance in the big dance halls.

***Derek Jones** from Ruthin remembers: "I loved dancing of any kind - old time, jive or rock and roll! I used to go to all the local dances but, as a real treat, when I'd saved up, I'd go to the dance at Reeces, on Parker Street, Liverpool on a Saturday night. I'd get the Crosville bus from Loggerheads to Woodside and then the ferry across the Mersey. It was fantastic as there were 3 dance floors and you used to go up in a lift, which was a novelty for me!"*

By bike

Merseyside was at the forefront of the growing interest in cycling in the late 19th century. Liverpool Velocipede Club became one of the first cycling clubs in Britain, established in 1869, soon after the first bicycle had been made! Anfield Bicycle Club, founded in 1879, gained a reputation as one of the greatest long distance cycling clubs and still remains active today. The Cyclists' Touring Club (CTC) Merseyside group was formed in 1895, and also still flourishes, organising a range of weekly rides.

Cycling grew rapidly in popularity during the first part of the 20th century. Cycling was the easiest and cheapest way for many city dwellers to get out into the countryside. Several other cycling groups were established in Merseyside with some focusing on racing and organising challenging 'Time Trials' races. The Liverpool Century Road Club, formed in 1916, was appropriately named as every member was expected to be able to cycle at least 100 miles in a day! The Mersey Roads Club was founded in 1924 for CTC members that were interested in racing. The Merseyside Wheelers, founded in 1933, focused on racing but also organised many day runs and camping weekends and became known as

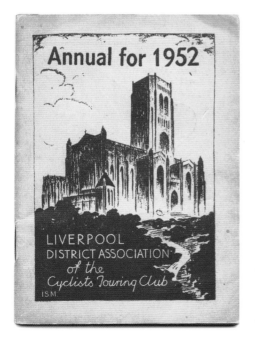

the 'marriage bureau' as it was one of the few mixed clubs! North Wales was a popular destination for club rides, catching the 8.15 or 8.45am ferry, cycling all day and catching the final 10.00pm ferry back. Even some of the more gentle social runs sound fairly gruelling to those of us unused to road cycling! For example an intermediate section ride crossed Llantysilio Mountain, with lunch in Llangollen and tea in Buckley, before riding back to the ferry!

Bob Williams comes from a cycling family. His father was a founder member of the Mersey Roads Club and Bob has followed in his father's footsteps. He remembers one

Following in Father's wheelmarks, is the all-cycling family of J. R. Williams, Mersey Roads Club. Locally the family is known as the Williams C.C.

The Williams family - four generations of cyclists

Courtesy of Bob Williams

particularly hair-raising incident: "In the 1950s we went on a ride to Ruthin with the Mersey Roads Club. I was riding on the back of a fixed wheel tandem, with my brother John on the front. It was hard work going up the hills on the tandem and we were getting left behind. We climbed up past the Clwyd Gate and started to descend the Bwlch to Ruthin, picking up speed in the hope of catching up. The front tyre burst on the hairpin bend, John jumped off, and the tandem continued into the hedge ahead with me sitting on the back. I was covered in thorns!"

Keen cyclist **Bob Nolan** describes the activities of the Time Triallists. "They would bolt their racing wheels onto special carriers and ride over to use courses such as the one at Rhydymwyn (long gone – now an industrial estate). Many would use B&Bs but hardy types would bed down under a hedge! In the morning they'd strip off the road tyres, lights and mudguards, bolt in the sprints and tubs (light wheels with tubular tyres), then don their racing clothes. Then it was a matter of riding 25, 50 or 100 miles against the clock, one at a time at one minute intervals, no taking pace or wheel-sucking! After that it was riding on for a bite of lunch, followed up with the ride home via circuitous route to get the miles in – up to 200 miles was a common diet for the strong men and women!"

Tandems at
Nant Alyn campsite

Courtesy of the
Morris family

As mentioned earlier, the great popularity of cycling into the Wirral and North Wales led to serious problems of overcrowding on the ferries. As a result the Merseyside CTC campaigned for cyclists to be allowed to use the Birkenhead Tunnel and on Saturday 21st July, 1934, the first cyclists rode enthusiastically through the tunnel. This widened the options for the keen cyclists but it added extra miles onto the ride and wasn't enjoyable so many still preferred to use the ferry.

> ***Ruth Williams*** *remembers coming through the tunnel as a passenger in the side-car of her parents' tandem. "The gears weren't working properly so my dad shouted to mum not to back pedal. Unfortunately mum misheard him, due to the noise in the tunnel, and stopped pedalling completely, leaving Dad to toil uphill out of the tunnel by himself! He didn't realise that she wasn't pedalling until a lorry of soldiers passed us, catcalling and laughing!"*

> ***May D'Arcy*** *cycled through the tunnel once on a youth club cycle ride to Loggerheads but did not enjoy the experience. "I was terrified going through the tunnel because of the noise and traffic and cried as I was cycling out!"*

David Backhouse, *a keen cyclist with the Merseyside Wheelers, fully understood May's comments:* "Cycling through the tunnel wasn't a pleasant experience on a fixed wheel bike. Going downhill you'd go very fast and, on one occasion, my chain came off. I had to coast downhill and then put the chain back on when I came to a standstill part-way up the hill, amidst the traffic noise and fumes!"

Bob Williams *recalls:* "Sometimes we cut it fine and missed the ferry. We would check the time on the Liver Building clock as we approached and, if we were too late, we would quickly use the tunnel, as the dock exit allowed traffic to enter at that time. We would pedal like mad through to Birkenhead and meet up with the rest of the club who had caught the ferry!"

Many cyclists organised their own rides. In those days families or small groups of youngsters often cycled into North Wales for a day. The first major challenge for any cyclist was the long ascent up Ewloe Hill from Queensferry and many also remember labouring up Rainbow Hill, Gwernymyndd on the way to Loggerheads.

David Backhouse on Ewloe Hill

Courtesy of David Backhouse

In the autumn *David Backhouse* *often cycled from Larkhill to Mold, aged 11 or 12, and filled his saddle-bag and butty-bag with conkers and sold them for 3 a penny (old money) back in Liverpool!"*

Ruth Williams *first cycled out on her own bike with her dad when she was 11.* "We stopped at the top of Ewloe Hill and I thought I was on top of the world!"

Derek Parsons *grew up in Penny Lane but now lives in Pantymwyn.* "I first came to the Loggerheads area after the war as a passenger, along with my brother, in the side car of our parents' tandem! I remember that they found it hard work pedalling up the Rainbow Hill, Gwernymynydd and sometimes had to get off and push! As a teenager I became a keen cyclist myself, joining the Cresta Wheelers, aged 13, and later the Liverpool Unity Cycling club. I cycled over from Liverpool many times."

Gordon Jones *recalls,* "I bought a second-hand Claud Butler racing bike soon *after my 13th birthday. It took a little while before I could persuade my parents to allow me to go as far as Loggerheads, but they eventually relented and I remember my initial struggles to get the bike up Rainbow Hill on my fixed wheel. There were no 27 geared machines in those days!"*

North Wales is still a popular destination for the cyclists, although the increased motor traffic, motorways and bypasses have changed the experience and impacted on many of the traditional routes. Off-road mountain biking has become extremely popular with younger cyclists but, during the summer, the lanes are still full of brightly clad groups of touring cyclists, and many of these groups still come from Merseyside.

A Mersey Wheelers ride along the Cheshire Lanes in the 1950s.

Courtesy of David Backhouse

GREETINGS FROM
LLANFERRES

THE VILLAGE

ENTRANCE TO FAIRY GLEN

THE PARISH CHURCH

The perfect holiday

For visitors from Merseyside, the countryside around Moel Famau and Loggerheads was a rural paradise. The heather clad hill-tops, sheep-grazed fields divided by stone walls, lush meadows with thick hedgerows, farming hamlets, picturesque villages and market towns, provided a complete contrast to the grime and bustle of the city. It must have been particularly appealing after the war when Merseyside was recovering from the intense bombing. In addition to the thousands who came on day trips, increasing numbers came to stay for weekends and longer holidays.

Camping and caravans

Intrepid youngsters used to camp at weekends or in the holidays, cycling from Liverpool or catching the bus, carrying all their equipment. Local farmers were often happy for youngsters or families to camp on their land, with livestock grazing nearby.

Angus Earps worked at JW Towers in Liverpool from the age of 14. "At the weekend, me and 2 friends loved to cycle to the Loggerheads area and camp. We'd usually come after work on a Friday and stay until Sunday. We camped up on the high ground above the woods on the opposite side of the road to The Druid at Llanferres and used to get milk from the local farm. We cooked

LHS. 49.   THE VILLAGE. LOGGERHEADS.

Postcard of Loggerheads

Courtesy of Denbighshire Countryside Service

44

on an open fire using steel bars on bricks to support our pans. Before we left, we buried the steel bars for safe keeping so we could use them next time! We brought some food with us from home but also bought extra bits from Llanferres shop. I remember buying my first glass of bitter in the Druid Inn (½ a pint), costing four pence h'penny!"

Some of the impromptu campsites developed gradually into more permanent sites, with farmers storing tents and equipment between visits and providing more facilities.

Nant Alyn *campsite at Rhydymwyn was one such site. The current owner,* **Ian Morris**, *recounts its history: "Campers first pitched their tents in the fields of my grandfather's smallholding at Nant Alyn Mill in the 1920s. It was very popular with cyclists coming to race at Rhydymwyn or using it as a base for touring and also with ramblers who had come on the train or bus. My grandfather used to go round with his pony and trap, collecting the camping fees. My grandmother ran a shop and cafe at the farm and, for a time, also offered bed and breakfast. They stored campers' equipment in an old tram and the site evolved gradually into something more permanent as huts, a railway carriage, 3 single-decker and 2 double-decker buses and a gypsy caravan were* placed or built in the fields. My father eventually took over the running of the site and now I run it with my wife Sue. In the early 1960s, when sites had to be registered, it became Leete Valley Caravan Park, evolving into the static caravan site it is today. Most of the caravans are still owned by families from Merseyside and some families have been visiting for 4 generations!

It was great growing up at Nant Alyn. I used to really look forward to the beginning of the season when all the families from Liverpool would arrive as the children were my friends and we'd play all summer long! I've grown up with many of the people who come to stay here - it's like a big extended family!"

Three generations of the Morris family have run Nant Alyn campsite

Courtesy of the
Morris family

46

Jack and Mavis Burns *have been coming to the site since the early 1950s. Jack recalls: "I first came to camp at Nant Alyn when I was 15, having got the bus to Rhydymwyn and walked from there. When I rounded the corner and first saw the valley my mouth dropped open. I couldn't believe how beautiful it was! I've been coming back ever since!"*

Mavis remembers: "I used to come here camping with my friends. We paid a penny for a sack of straw to sleep on in the tents and the girls and boys always had to be in separate tents! After we were married we stayed in a home-made cabin, built from the back of an old lorry that just had 2 bunks at one end and a paraffin stove for cooking. Once we arrived with our 2 week old daughter and Mrs Morris gave us a cupboard drawer for her to sleep in."

Most campers came back regularly, so it became a real community. Mr and Mrs Morris kept an eye on the younger folk, helping them out and ensuring that moral standards were kept up! Solid friendships were made and also several marriages resulted from meetings at Nant Alyn.

Jack remembers, "Mrs Mac, who had one of the wooden shacks, always had a pan of scouse (lamb stew) on the go and would offer it to everybody! My brother Jimmy used to cycle out regularly and camp. It was here that he first met Paula, who became his wife, as she camped here with her friend."

Alan Cockerton recalls how he first found Nant Alyn: "My dad owned a motorbike shop in Birkenhead so I rode motorbikes from an early age. I first came to Rhydymwyn in the 1960s to compete in the off-road motorbike trials that were held every weekend through the winter. I found the campsite by chance and loved the location immediately - it was like entering another world."

Margaret Thompson, from Bootle, first came as a child in the 1960s, staying in one of the double-decker buses. "I bought a caravan here 5 years ago and have enjoyed bringing my own children and grandchildren to stay. It's great to see them enjoying doing the same things that I loved to do as a child - having the freedom to explore the woods, building dens, playing on rope swings and going on long walks. Today's youngsters, growing up in the city, rarely get a chance to do things like these."

Alick Stark has a 68 year association with Nant Alyn, having first explored the valley when he stayed at Gwernaffield as an evacuee! "After the war the family returned to Liverpool, but I never forgot the Alyn Valley and returned often to stay at Nant Alyn camp. I would finish work on a Friday and head home to pick up my wife and 3 children. We had a motorcycle and sidecar - my wife would sit behind me and the children and luggage would be in the sidecar. Sometimes the journey would take up to 2 hours. We had a wooden shack on the campsite with a stable door on it. Each time we came I brought pieces of wood and added bits onto the shack!"

Parc Farm caravan site, set in stunning countryside just outside Llanarmon-yn Iâl, has been running for over 50 years. Like Nant Alyn, it began as an informal campsite with holiday-makers asking the farmer if they could use his field. During the 1960s, touring caravans became popular and the campsite expanded gradually to the large site for static and touring caravans that it is today.

The site has not lost its appeal for Merseysiders as owner, **Jane Evans**, explains: "Over 60% of our visitors are from Merseyside with some going back 2 or 3 generations. Some of the folk who originally came here camping or touring are now coming back and buying static caravans in retirement for their families to enjoy."

Patricia Condliff, from Greasby, is a long-standing visitor. "I've been coming to Parc Farm for 40 years – over half my life! I love the peace and quiet here without constant traffic noise and police sirens."

Betty Keller, from Maghull, has brought 3 generations of her family to Parc Farm. "I've always felt an affinity with Wales - my father was from Fishguard and my mother's maiden name was Jones. As children, we always came for holidays to North Wales and, when we had children of our own, we regularly drove to Loggerheads for a day out and also spent holidays touring Wales in a caravan."

Her daughter, **Annette Dooley**, recalls: "To be honest, as a kid, I wasn't keen to go out to Wales each Sunday as I wanted to play with my friends in the park! However, once we got there I really enjoyed the walks and came

Relaxing at Nant Alyn

Courtesy of the
Morris family

50

to love the outdoor life. As an adult, I've brought my own children out here many times."

In addition to the larger campsites, there were numerous wooden huts, caravans and even old railway carriages nestled in the valleys around Moel Famau that were available to rent. Most modern holiday-makers, used to en suite bathrooms and modern luxuries, would turn their noses up at the primitive conditions in the wooden shacks, but they were a dream destination for many Merseyside families and young people, giving them a real taste of outdoor life. Holiday tastes changed during the 1970s, particularly when cheaper air travel made holidays abroad affordable for ordinary folk, and the numbers coming to stay in North Wales declined so many of the huts fell gradually into ruin."

Betty Earps has happy memories of staying with her family in a gypsy caravan near Llanferres. "It was so exciting when we got to our little caravan in the field, surrounded by horses and cows. You couldn't see it from the road as it was tucked in a corner of the field and hidden by thick hedges. I remember one old horse that liked to rub itself on the caravan chimney!

Mum cooked on a little range in the caravan and we all used to gather wood to keep it going. The smell of wood smoke still reminds me of that little caravan.

At the gypsy caravan, Llanferres

Courtesy Betty Earps

I'll always remember the crystal clear stream water in the field, running over pebbles. We filled jugs with water from the stream and poured it into a big bowl in the caravan. We used to wash in it but it was clean enough to drink too. I also remember walking to the nearby farm to collect eggs and buttermilk in enamel jugs. They were happy times!"

Anne Woodward *from Tafarn-y-Gelyn remembers the wooden chalet behind her parents' farm. "The original owners were a Liverpool family who used it themselves but also let it out to other families. Later, my parents bought it and continued to let it until the early 1970s. It was just a simple wooden hut mounted on a brewer's dray. It was very small, with just a central living room and a tiny bedroom at each end, but later they built extensions on stilts to give it a separate kitchen, a washroom and a larger bedroom!"*

Derek Parsons *has fond memories of numerous idyllic weekends and holidays spent with his parents and younger brother around Pantymwyn and Loggerheads. "Sometimes we would camp on a farm, bringing our bell tent and equipment with us on the bus, but later we rented rooms above the Colomendy pub and, on many occasions, rented an old railway carriage in Cefn Bychan Wood."*

Pat Hughes' *family lived in West Derby but loved the Loggerheads area and often came for day trips when Pat was a child. In the late 50s, they had*

At Fairy Glen

Courtesy of Derek Parsons

Staying at Cefn Bychan Wood

Courtesy of Derek Parsons

a caravan near the tea-gardens at Loggerheads and kept it there until about 1980. "The caravan was situated in a beautiful spot on a stretch of open field beside the river. We used water from the river in the caravan and never had any illnesses. We all loved it there and used to go as often as we could. In time we brought our own children there too. It was equally popular with family friends, and several couples even spent their honeymoon there!"

Frank Kennedy and 3 or 4 friends from Toxteth used to love going 'barning'. "We'd cycle into North Wales at weekends and ask farmers if we could stay overnight in one of their barns. Most of the farmers were kind to us city lads but one couple in Corwen were exceptional. The farmer's wife showed us the barn and soon reappeared with drinking chocolate and hot food. The next morning she asked us to wash ourselves in the trough in the yard and then led us into the kitchen for a huge breakfast of bacon and eggs, all from the farm. They wouldn't take any money from us."

Ross Cameron's family from Hooton came regularly for holidays to Nercwys in the late 1950s and 60s. "My father was a founder member of Merseyside Model Aircraft Club and they sometimes used an old shepherd's cottage on

Ivan Cameron on Nercwys Mountain, circa 1940s

Courtesy of Ross Cameron

the top of Nercwys Mountain as a base for flying events. Later, dad rented the cottage for family holidays and, although it was very basic by today's standards, I have wonderful memories of the happy times we spent there. It was a long walk from the bus stop across the moors up to the cottage, especially for my dad who carried my little sister on his shoulders with a big suitcase in each hand! We children used to walk down the hill each day to fetch water from the well and we also visited our aunt who lived in a thatched cottage on the outskirts of the village.

Trees now cover the mountain and only ruins of the cottage remain but I can still clearly picture it silhouetted in the moonlight on the mountain top alongside a solitary tree."

Family holidays at Nercwys

Courtesy of Ross Cameron

Pat Gore recalls staying with her parents in a cottage in the hills above Nannerch in 1952, when she was 11. "The cottage just had 2 large rooms, one downstairs and one upstairs. Cooking and heating were done with a range and there was no electricity, running water or sewage system. There was a shed attached to the cottage. Just inside the shed door was a recess with a plank of wood across. The plank had a hole in it and a bucket beneath it – this was the toilet!"

In the late 1950s and early 1960s, **Ron Plummer**, from Litherland, used to enjoy holidays staying with relatives in Lixwm, near Mold. "It was here that I developed my passion for the countryside and walking. I thought nothing of walking for miles on the quiet lanes."

Nancy Willan's parents fell in love with Cilcain when they stayed there on their honeymoon in 1915 and returned for several more visits, before finally buying Hillside Cottage in the 1930s. Nancy recalls: "Those pre-war years were pleasant. We would spend weekends at the cottage, carrying everything we needed to Penny Lane to catch the tramcar to Pier Head, then the ferry to Birkenhead, a Crosville bus to Loggerheads or Pantymwyn and finally a walk to Cilcain. "

Below left: Pat Gore collecting water at Nannerch

Courtesy of Pat Gore

Below right: Ron Plummer at Lixwm

Courtesy of Ron Plummer

David Collinson used to spend happy holidays in his grandparents' cottage, The Nook, in Cilcain. "My grandfather went to Cilcain to visit his sister-in-law after her son had drowned tragically. He must have been very taken with the area as he ended up buying a cottage there himself in 1910. He was a wine merchant in Liverpool and perhaps thought the cottage was a good place to entertain his clients and to take the family for breaks. At first they used to travel by train from Crosby via Chester and Mold to arrive at Star Crossing, 2 miles out of the village. From here they were taken by horse and trap to the cottage."

Maeshafn Youth Hostel

Merseysiders were at the forefront of developing cheap and simple accommodation for walkers and cyclists. Liverpool and District Ramblers' Federation established the Youth Hostels Association in 1929, supported by the Merseyside Cyclists' Touring Club, and the first youth hostels they opened were in North Wales.

Maeshafn Youth Hostel opened in 1931. It was the first purpose-built hostel, designed by Clough Williams-Ellis, who is best known for creating Portmeirion village. It was funded mainly by Merseyside benefactors, including a generous

donation from the Holt family of Sudeley House, and provided a welcome overnight stay for walkers, cyclists, Guide, Scout and youth groups.

Maeshafn Youth Hostel

Courtesy of Denbighshire Records Office

Many families of cyclists took every opportunity to come over, using the youth hostels to extend and link their mileage. Maeshafn and Cyffylliog were popular stopovers in the pre and post-war days but holiday habits have changed and Cyffylliog closed in the 1950s and Maeshafn more recently in 2005.

Maidie Brown *has fond memories of her stays at Maeshafn as a Ranger Guide. "It was basic but comfortable built mainly of wood with three-tiered bunks and lit by oil lamps, situated on a hill, Moel Findeg, surrounded by birch trees."*

Keen cyclist *Ruth Williams* *and her family have a long association with Maeshafn Youth Hostel. "I first stayed when I was 11 on a cycling trip with my dad. Until then I had ridden a tandem with my dad and this was my first long trip on my own bike so it was very special. Since then, Bob and I have stayed several times on cycling trips with our own family, and have hired the whole hostel when organising a 2-day Road Race for the cycling club. My younger son, David, even held his stag night there during one of the road races!"*

Paying guests

Before and after the Second World War, many farms and houses in the villages took in paying guests in the summer for some extra money. In some cases the family were often squeezed into one room or barn to make room for the paying guests!

Eirwyn Rogers remembers his mother taking in visitors at their house in Llanarmon-yn-Iâl during the 1940s and 50s. "The same families used to come back every year. They would stay for a week, getting the Crosville bus to Mold and then another to Llanarmon. My mother used to take them on walks to show them the area. I enjoyed chatting with one of the fathers as, although our

Roy and Ruth Preston and other visitors at Maeshafn Youth Hostel

Courtesy of Ruth Williams

59

lives were very different, we both worked with horses - he was a docker using them to move cargo and I worked for the forestry using horses to move felled timber."

Olga Thomas *was brought up at Bryn Tirion, Maeshafn, and has strong memories of the Merseyside visitors who used to come and stay during the 1930s and 40s. "During the summer we often had paying guests, or 'visitors' as mum called them. Sometimes they booked in advance, but occasionally we would take cyclists at the last minute when Maeshafn Youth Hostel was full. I remember going to bed in my own bedroom and waking up on the sofa as I'd been carried down in the evening so that my bed could be used by a late arrival! When we were a bit older, my brother and I would often take visitors up Moel Famau, acting as their guides for the day."*

Bryn Tirion was later owned by a butcher from the Wirral who used it for holidays but is now, once again, offering accommodation for visitors, many of whom still come from the Liverpool and the Wirral.

Sylvia Hughes, the present owner, comments: "It's hard to imagine a family of visitors being put up in the original cottage as it was tiny. We've extended the cottage a lot since Olga lived here to provide more spacious guest accommodation, but our visitors still come for the peace and natural beauty of the area, just as they did in Olga's childhood."

Please be sure to send your child
with a packed bag and the
GAS MASK (in box) at 9 o'clock.

Children must come
to school this morning
and this afternoon as
usual.
Scholars will not be taken
to the station today,
but what you can in the
bags and don't wor...

Evacuees - Fleeing
the bombs

Chapter 4

In spring 1939, when the outbreak of the Second World War seemed inevitable, it was recognised quickly that Liverpool was likely to be a prime target for Hitler's bombers as its port was of vital importance.

Plans were put rapidly into place for the mass evacuation of schoolchildren from the areas most at risk of bombing to rural reception areas in England and North Wales. The evacuation scheme was offered to school age children and mothers with children under 5. It was non-compulsory except where areas needed to be cleared of civilians for military or other reasons. The government was to bear the initial cost of evacuation but evacuees whose families could afford to contribute to their maintenance had to do so. By the time war was declared many thousands of Merseyside children were ready for evacuation, either with their schools or through private arrangements made by their parents.

School evacuation

Many schoolchildren moved with their schools, in groups in the charge of their teachers. During the spring and summer, schools held meetings for parents to prepare them for the possibility of evacuation. On 31st August 1939, an evacuation instruction was issued to all schools on the evacuation list and notices for parents were posted outside schools, giving details of the timings and procedures to be followed.

Between 1st and 6th September, 226 special evacuation trains left Liverpool, providing places for 150,000 children and adults. In reality, only 95,000 places were actually taken, as many changed their minds at the last minute. About 44,000 Merseyside evacuees went to North Wales, including many to Denbighshire and Flintshire.

An equal amount of forward planning took place in the selected reception areas and the work relied heavily upon the input of large numbers of volunteers. As soon as the evacuation was announced, the Chief Reception Officer and his team of billeting officers began work. Billeting officers were issued with lists of accommodation, billeting allowance forms and emergency rations. Volunteers put individual quotas of biscuits, milk and chocolate into carrier bags and prepared bedding for despatch. The numbers and constituents of evacuee groups often varied considerably from the details that had been sent to the billeting officers, causing endless organisational problems as areas expecting mainly school age children were sent young mothers with babies and vice versa!

School evacuation

Courtesy of Liverpool Record Office, Liverpool Libraries

Please be sure to send your c____
with a packed bag and the
GAS MASK (in box) at 9 o'clock

Children must com__
to school this morning
and this afternoon as
usual.
Scholars will not be tak__
to the station today.
Put what you can in the
bags and don't worry

Finding a Billet

On arrival at an evacuation centre billeting forms for each evacuee were completed along with a medical inspection. Emergency rations were issued and each group was accompanied to their billets. In some areas the distribution centre had allocated children to specific billets and had attempted to place the evacuees in the better households, avoiding drunks, debtors, women of easy virtue etc! At other distribution centres, it was more of a cattle market, with billets keen to take the cleanest, prettiest or strongest child. Whilst some were lucky, this method could be very distressing for the evacuees and inevitably left a group of unwanted children.

Lister Drive School were evacuated en masse to Ruthin Rural District and several former pupils have contributed their memories.

Evacuation assembly point

Courtesy of Liverpool Record Office, Liverpool Libraries

17th March 1939

Meeting for parents about the evacuation scheme

August 29th 1939

Registration suspended and an Evacuation Rehearsal took place

3rd September 1939

Children evacuated to Mold Rural District

Nov 27th 1939

Two teachers recalled for home teaching but later sent back to help with evacuees

Butler Street
School log-book

Courtesy of Liverpool Record
Office, Liverpool Libraries

On next page:
Evacuees boarding
the train including
pupils from Sacred
Heart School, Low
Hill

Courtesy of Liverpool Record
Office, Liverpool Libraries

Angus Earps recalls: *"On the day the whole school was evacuated, we went to school with our packed bags, gas masks and identity labels, and all the children took the bus from Green Lane to the station and then the train to Ruthin. A bus took us to Ruthin Town Hall where we were sorted into groups to go to the outlying villages. Each child was given 2 tins of corned beef and a tin of Libby's milk to give to their hosts!"*

Laurence Lloyd recalls: *"On arrival we all had to stand around waiting for our names to be called out. At times it seemed like a cattle auction, being picked out in ones or twos to join a family."*

Vivienne Shimmin, who was 10 at the time, was one of the fortunate ones: *"We were taken to Llanfair D C Village Hall and had to sit down while local people walked round the room choosing the children they wanted. My mum had made sure that my 7 year old sister, Doreen, and I were clean and tidy and we were dressed in identical dresses with pink ducks so probably looked quite sweet. Miss Jones from Plas Tirion chose us. She was very wealthy and we couldn't believe it when her chauffeur took us to the limousine to drive us to her home!"*

Others were less fortunate. **Billy Moffitt** and his brothers, **John** and **Harry**, were evacuated later, after their house was destroyed by a bomb. Billy recalls waiting to be billeted: *"We were sent by train to Ruthin and gathered in the Town Hall along with many other children. Here the billeting officers tried to find homes for all the children and local people turned up to choose their evacuees. Most householders only wanted to take 1 or 2 children so us 3 brothers were the last to be chosen."*

Pat Hartley was evacuated from Birkenhead to Towyn with her elder brother, **Robert**, and her little sister, **Audrey**, at the outbreak of war. *"Mum had made Robert promise to look after us and he took this very seriously, refusing to let anyone separate us. At Towyn, nobody wanted to take 3 children and the policeman, who had been driving us round all day to try and find us a*

billet, was despairing by nightfall as no home had been found for us. He eventually took us to his own house, just for that night. However, his wife took to us and persuaded him to let us stay. They were very kind and we stayed there for 2 or 3 years."

Whilst there are stories of unwilling hosts who didn't treat their evacuees well, and evacuees who encountered prejudice, there are a wealth of heart-warming stories, both from Liverpudlians who remember the kindness shown to them, and from Welsh folk who describe their efforts to make the evacuees feel at home and who felt real concern for what the youngsters were suffering.

Above: Robert, Pat and Audrey Hartley

Left: Robert, Pat and Audrey playing happily in their billet

Courtesy of Pat Hartley

Billy Moffitt *and his brothers had mixed experiences as they were moved numerous times from private homes and hostels during their time at Ruthin but he particularly remembers the kindness shown to them in one billet. "Mrs*

Jones took all 3 of us for a short while, although she didn't have much space. We lived alongside her 18 year old daughter, Megan, and her sons, Tom and Edwin, who were similar ages to us. Mrs Jones was a great lady and they made us very welcome. Megan used to take us down to the Scout field and play football with us. All 3 of us became choirboys at St Peter's Church along with Tom and Edwin. We can still sing the Welsh national anthem !"

Vivienne Shimmin *loved her time staying in relative luxury at Plas Tirion. "Miss Jones was very kind to me and Doreen and let our* brother, Ralph, join us too. We stayed for 5 years and, when our parents came to visit, she put them up in a grand four-poster bed! There was plenty of food as there was a farm close by and Miss Jones made bread every day. At first there were servants but they soon left to join the war effort so we helped in the house and on the farm."

Whilst North East Wales was not a direct target for bombing and locals did not feel directly under fire, there were clear views across to Liverpool from many places and so the nightly bombing of the city was seen on a regular basis. Many have described this and it may account for the depth of concern expressed by local folk who had dealings with the evacuees.

Dilys Williams, who was a young teenager at the time, recalls looking after 2 very young evacuees: "I remember the day that the evacuees from Liverpool came to our village of Llanddoged very well. It was the beginning of September 1939 and I had been down to the village after lunch on an errand. I saw Mr. Davies, our school's headmaster, who asked me whether my mother would take some of the children. I told him to bring 2 little girls and hurried home to tell my mam the news. Around 5 pm Mr. Jones' car arrived bringing two

Choirboys Ruthin church (Billy Moffit is 4th from left and John 2nd from right)

Courtesy of Billy Moffitt

5 year old girls, one with dark hair and one fair. They were very subdued and quiet, their names written on a little square piece of paper, which had been tied securely to their coats with safety pins. They had gas masks on their backs and their clothes were in parcels wrapped with brown paper tied up with string. In their hands, they carried small paper bags that contained biscuits and tins of corned beef.

My job was to look after them. They would go to bed with me, which was sometimes a bit of an ordeal as they found this time of day the hardest. They would be crying and I'm sure I cried a bit myself as my English wasn't very good! After a while things got a bit better, we would sing and say prayers after going to bed. You would be surprised at how many prayers they knew – prayers were every song such as 'My Bonnie lies over the Ocean', 'Shenandoah', 'Lambeth Walk' and 'Bobby Shafto' - and then we would say 'God Bless' everyone before going to sleep! When the bombing subsided the evacuees returned home. I wonder what happened to those 2 little girls? I hope I managed to help them a little bit during their time of missing home and that my home was of some comfort to them."

Tony Jones, who was a pupil at Ysgol Llanferres during the war recalls: "When they started bombing Liverpool, mothers and children would come to stay out here. Old houses, caravans and shacks were done up for them to live in. Once they were settled, the children came to our school so there was a mixture of Scousers and Welsh. Occasionally there was the odd misunderstanding. Welsh went to one side at that time. It wasn't a problem as we knew what they'd been through in Liverpool – they had to come to the country. We all got on fine together once we got to know one another."

Elizabeth Bamber lived in the White Horse pub, St Asaph. "In 1939, when I was 14, my mother and father agreed to care for two 12 year old boys who were evacuated from St Francis Xavier's College. I was delighted to see them as my brother had recently died, my other 2 brothers had joined the Army and my 2 sisters were in the Royal Air Force so I was the only one left at home. I remember the boys arriving at our house wearing their school uniform - lovely red blazers and grey trousers. Their parents visited every other Sunday and the boys stayed with us for years. I often wonder what happened to them."

Pat Gore was born in Denbigh while her parents were evacuated and spent her early years staying with Mrs Addie at her shop in Denbigh before moving

[FOR USE BY SCHOOL MANAGERS.]

CITY OF LIVERPOOL.

EDUCATION COMMITTEE.

The Lesser Brethren
(M. W. Tarrant)

Butler Street Council **SCHOOL**

Girls' Department.

Liverpool, 6.

April 26th, 1945.

Dear Friends in the Reception Area of Cilcain,

Although several years have passed since our large party of scholars and teachers were so warmly welcomed into Cilcain, the memory of your kindness during those uncertain days still lives with us.

We send this small token of our appreciation of the kindly affection and attention of the foster parents, and other friends, who received us into their homes, of the consideration and welcome extended to us by the Head Teacher and Staff of the School, for the opportunity of joining in worship in the Churches, Chapels and Sunday Schools, and for the many kindnesses shown to us by various friends who organised the welfare of our large party.

May the coming peace reveal to us all, the meaning of these strange times.

In appreciation of many happy days,

From the Scholars and Staff of

Butler Street Girls' School.

to Gronant. She recalls Mrs Addie with great fondness: "I called Mrs Addie 'Nana' and, even after we had moved to Gronant, we used to go back regularly to visit her. She used to give me 'garibaldi' or 'fig roll' biscuits from the glass-topped display bins!"

Whilst most evacuees talk of the kindness they encountered a few evacuees did encounter prejudice.

Nancy Willan recalls: *"A few of the Welsh pupils looked askance at we 'intruders', and we suffered some bad times. Once, when having to write an essay on 'Our Class', one lad wrote, 'in our class we have a teacher, boys, girls and evacuees.' One day I was tormented so much that I hit back and clouted a couple of these lads while the art teacher's back was turned. They never tried it again!'*

Sheila Williams had fled with her family to Mold to escape the May Blitz. "We had a mixed welcome. Some shopkeepers were very kind but others didn't want to serve us and some people nicknamed us 'bomb dodgers'."

Pat Gore outside Mrs Addie's shop

Courtesy of Pat Gore

Private evacuees

Some families sorted out their own accommodation, sending children to stay with relatives or people they found through personal contacts in Wales. Others moved as a family (excluding the fathers who were usually in the forces or stayed in the city to work) renting cottages or lodgings in safe rural areas. A few of the more affluent owned holiday homes in Wales and used these for evacuation.

Pat Hartley remembers: *"Audrey and I were evacuated a second time when Birkenhead began to be bombed, this time to Derwen Cottage in Cilcain. My parents knew William Davies, who lived there with his wife Hannah, as he worked in Birkenhead looking after the horses used by British Rail. My parents paid a sum to Mr and Mrs Davies to look after us. We went to the local school and also to Capel Gad and learned Welsh verses each week for Sunday School. We loved the open countryside around Cilcain and have many happy memories of playing outdoors."*

Margaret Whalley recalls: *"I was evacuated to Pontblyddyn, to stay with*

74

the Roberts' family. My uncle worked at a timber yard in Liverpool driving wagons of timber to Padeswood in North Wales. When the bombing started my uncle brought me, my 5 siblings, my mum and grandad in the timber wagon to Padeswood each night and took us back to Liverpool each morning! After a week or so Mr Roberts, who was night-watchman at the Padeswood yard, offered to look after me and my sister. They were really kind to us and I stayed for 4 years, firstly attending Pontblyddyn primary school and then the secondary school in Mold. I enjoyed the field trips from school to Moel Famau and the Leete and was also lucky enough to stay with my friend's auntie in Cilcain during the school holidays."

David Collinson's grandparents owned a cottage in Cilcain. "When war broke out my mother, sister, grandmother, aunt and I moved to the cottage in Cilcain, leaving father working in Liverpool. My mother, along with the parents of 2 other evacuee families, set up a small private school in a room in the Vicarage, taught by a newly qualified teacher from St Asaph. Perhaps there were too many of us to go to the village school, or perhaps our parents worried we wouldn't fit in. Some of the older children were studying for school certificate so were too old for the village school anyway. The school only lasted for 6 months as the bombing didn't start and so we returned to Liverpool. My aunt stayed in the cottage throughout the war, as her house in Crosby was being used by a family whose home had been bombed. During the week she walked 2 miles to Pantymwyn to catch the bus into Liverpool from so she could open her café on Old Hall Street to serve lunches to the office workers!"

Alan Roach was only 4 when he had to be evacuated with his mother, grandmother and 2 younger sisters, after their house in Aigburth was severely damaged by a landmine in May 1941. Family friends near Ruthin tried to find somewhere for them but it was hard to place such a big family. Eventually Major Bromhead, a widower who lived in a large house called Plas Drâw at Llangynhafal, near Ruthin, was persuaded to take them, although he wasn't keen to have a family with young children. There were maids, gardeners and even a chauffeur and the estate also included a farm! Alan recalls: "I think I was overawed at first as it was such a big house. We had to stay in our

Pat and Audrey Hartley walking to school in Cilcain

Courtesy of Pat Hartley

quarters and didn't have the run of the whole house but our quarters alone were far bigger than the whole of our house in Liverpool! I quickly settled in and began to enjoy myself. Most of the staff were soon conscripted and my mum took over the running of the household. She worked very hard but, for us children, it was paradise and by the time we had to go back to Liverpool in 1945, we didn't want to leave.

We always had plenty of food including superb vegetables and soft fruit from the gardens – strawberries, raspberries, yellow gooseberries – lots of things that we hadn't had before in Liverpool! They also kept chickens so we had a supply of eggs. The gardeners shot rabbits and wood pigeons so they were often on the menu and, when we first arrived, there were occasionally shooting parties on the estate. The shot pheasants were hung in a big room with gauze windows at the back of the house. We also picked bilberries, blackberries and wild cherries."

Barbara Burrows *from Bootle was 5 when war broke out. Bootle was a prime target for bombing so her father rented a small bungalow at Bryn Eglwys and Barbara moved there with her mum and sister. "At first I went to Bryn Eglwys School but after a while all the evacuees were taught in the village hall by an English teacher as we weren't learning anything in Welsh. I liked it at Bryn Eglwys as I made good friends with the girl from the farm next door and we had wonderful food from all the farm produce! My mum found it hard though as she'd left a 3-bedroomed house with running water, a flushing toilet, electricity and good public transport and moved to a tiny bungalow in a small Welsh village with a chemical toilet, water that had to be collected from a well and no electricity!"*

Anne Woodward *of Tafarn-y-Gelyn, near Loggerheads, recalls the sad story of the Martin family who owned a little wooden chalet in the field by her family's farm: "When war broke, out Mrs Martin and her children, Edna and Paul, moved from Liverpool to the chalet but Mr Martin remained in the city to work. He was killed in an air raid when he was helping an elderly neighbour whose house was directly hit."*

Viv Haworth *has very happy memories of her evacuation to Denbigh. "When the war started my mum and 3 sisters decided to move out of the city with us 7 children. We lodged at Copy Farm, near Denbigh, occupying the front room and one bedroom that had 3 double beds in it. The farmers, the Tudors, made us very welcome and my brother, sister, cousins and I loved playing with their*

Plas Drâw

Courtesy of Alan Roach

Happy times at Copy Farm

Courtesy of Viv Howarth

children. Mum and my aunts helped with haymaking and other jobs on the farm while us young children would play. Shire horses were used to pull the ploughs and other farm machinery and I remember being lifted onto a shire horse for a ride as it was coming back from the field. I couldn't believe how high it was!

*My cousin **Reg Blore** was born near Denbigh during our stay at Copy Farm. He became a footballer, playing for Liverpool, and because of his Welsh birthplace, also played for Wales Under 20s.*

I think we had a much better time than some other evacuees as we were well fed with the farm produce and fruit from the orchard; we were with our mothers and cousins, and were treated so warmly by our Welsh hosts."

Educating the evacuees

The Local Education Authorities in the reception areas were responsible for the education of the evacuees they received. This posed a particular problem for Welsh schools that had to deal with language issues as well as lack of space, as Welsh was the commonly spoken language in the playground and often in the classroom.

Some schools ran a double shift system, teaching Welsh children in the mornings and the evacuees in the afternoon. In other areas, when teachers had come with their evacuees, they were given their own makeshift schoolrooms in local village halls or chapels. At first there were teething troubles sorting out accommodation for the evacuees and their teachers.

Sept 5th

A communication was received stating that all the schools in the county were to close until 11th September to receive evacuees from Liverpool. Local children were not to attend school until the evacuees had been medically examined.

Sept 13th

There are 30 evacuees attending school this week under the charge 2 of their teachers. Some of the school stock has been given to them and they are permitted to use the school equipment.

Sept 18th

The Pentre Celyn scholars attended school all day today as the evacuee children were accommodated in the local chapel schoolroom.

Sept 19th

The evacuee children occupied the school today as Liverpool Education Committee hadn't sanctioned the alternative accommodation. Dr Thomas, HMI, called this morning and suggested that the evacuees could be given one of the classrooms so that the school could run normally.

Sept 22nd

The local children have attended school 3 days this week. Today (Friday) the evacuees have been given the infant classroom and work will now be carried out normally except that the infants are sharing a classroom with Standards I, II and III.

Log-book entry from Ysgol Pentre Celyn

Courtesy of Laurence Lloyd

Despite the efforts of the Welsh schools and the Merseyside teachers, education was extremely disrupted for many youngsters during the war.

Nancy Willan had passed the scholarship in 1939 but was then evacuated with her school to Holywell. After a short while she returned to Liverpool but, when the bombing began in earnest, Nancy and her mother went to stay in the family's holiday cottage in Cilcain. She recalls: "There was no room for me at the Alun Grammar School in Mold at first, so I spent a year at Cilcain village school. By the time I began at the Alun, I had missed nearly 2 years of secondary education, including the time at Holywell and in the Blitz, so had to work hard to make up lost time."

John Pascoe was one of many whose education was curtailed by the war. "I was originally evacuated with St Francis Xavier's College to St Asaph for about 18 months. We went to the local school and were taught partly by the small number of Jesuit teachers who had come with us and also by local teachers. Later, my cousins and I went to live with my grandmother in Rhyl where she had rented a house to keep us all away from the bombing. I went to the local secondary school and joined in most of the lessons except for Welsh. During Welsh lessons we were given jobs like gardening to do as I don't think they had spare teachers for us. I left school at 14 and got a job. This was what was expected of us as there was a shortage of labour and the schools were overcrowded and understaffed due to the war. With hindsight, I regret my lack of education but I didn't at the time as getting a job was a great adventure!"

For others, education continued to a high standard, despite the disruption,

Barbara Adams from Lister Drive School remembers: "We were taught at Salem chapel, Llanfair DC by our own teachers who showed great kindness and did a good job of teaching us in difficult circumstances. I sat the Liverpool City Scholarship in the altar of the chapel, leaning on the pulpit, and passed! First I went to Bryn Hyfryd (the Grammar School in Ruthin) and learned a lot of Welsh there. I stayed for about 5 years before going back to Liverpool to finish my schooling."

Some children, particularly the private evacuees or those that stayed a long time, went to the local schools and became fully integrated and fluent in Welsh.

Private evacuee Alan Roach recalls: "When I reached school age I went to Gellifor school, walking from Plas Drâw, with 3 brothers from Everton who

were billeted at a nearby farm. I enjoyed school and used to play with the local children. We were allowed to speak English in class if we needed to but soon picked up Welsh."

Harry Moffitt *spent 10 years in North Wales and grew to love it. "I arrived with my 2 brothers when I was 5 and, at first, moved billets several times in and around Ruthin. Later, I was billeted at Derwen Llannerch Farm, Pentre Celyn, and became very settled. The farmer looked after me very well and I loved working on the farm, bringing the cattle in and collecting the eggs. I went to Pentre Celyn School and, at first, some of the children gave me a hard time, teasing me about being an evacuee. I remember having a fight in the playground with one boy. We both got 'six of the best' off the headmaster for it but became good friends after that! I became fluent in Welsh as that was the language spoken all around me, at home, in the village and at school. I assumed I'd go home at 14 when I finished school but the headmaster wanted me to sit exams for Wrexham Tech as I was top of the class – even in Welsh! I passed the exams and studied at Wrexham for 2 years with a view to training as an engineer."*

Nancy Willan feeding a lamb

Courtesy of Nancy Willan

Country Life

Rural life suited most of the evacuees who enjoyed the freedom of the open countryside and the natural world around them. The children who ended up on farms, especially boys, seemed to thrive, enjoying helping with the livestock and the outdoor life.

Billy Moffitt *recalls: "Fetching the cows home every night was a delight – you got them all moving and you hitched a ride on the back of one by catching hold of its tail and you were pulled up. No stops, no bells, no on, no off!"*

Nancy Willan *recalls helping on a local farm: "After the corn was brought in from the fields it was stored in the barns. We children helped gather the sheaves as they were tossed down to be taken to the thresher. One day, as I bent over, an escaping mouse landed on my neck. Everyone screamed except me! I used to help churning butter and was rewarded with a tiny pat of the precious stuff. It was hard work and I don't think my right arm ever recovered."*

Gerald Black and his brother, **Brian**, were evacuated to Llay, near Wrexham. "We had to share a camp-bed which was problematic as we had to make sure the other one didn't fall out! The best thing was that our hosts had a horse and cart mobile fish and chip shop! We also loved catching rabbits with ferrets playing in the River Alyn!"

Laurence Lloyd was delighted with his second billet on a farm: "I immensely enjoyed life on the farm, helping with milking cows by hand, feeding pigs, hens, geese and ducks, also helping to muck out and be a helpful farm-hand. Harvest time was great fun, each farmer helping another at threshing time."

Angus Earps stayed in Llanelidan for a year and loved the rural life. "I stayed with Mrs Clayton, the postwoman, who delivered the post on foot and lived opposite the village shop. I used to help in the shop, going round in the delivery van to all the outlying farms. They used to deliver groceries to the farms and buy eggs from the farms to sell back in the shop. I also remember going to get bulk seed and delivering that to the farms and helping with threshing grain when the threshing machine

went from farm to farm. There were pheasants everywhere and there were regular shoots. One of the gamekeepers lodged in the same house and I learned a bit about gamekeeping."

Pat Gore has strong memories of growing up at Gronant, on the coast. "Gronant was very rural and quiet. I remember my mother taking me out in my pram for walks. We would often come across a herd of cows being moved from one field to another. Sometimes a bull would be in the middle of the herd with a sack over his head! Sheep would get into the garden if we left the gate open overnight. We grew lots of vegetables and fruit. I used to be sent out with a basket to collect peas for lunch. I loved peas so a lot of the pods would be half-empty when I took them in!"

Settling into village life

Most of the evacuees who came to give their memories had very happy memories of the time they spent in North Wales. They played with the Welsh children and some made lasting friendships although there was often great rivalry between Welsh and English kids at sport, particularly soccer!

Community life revolved around the church or chapel and most Welsh families were very devout. In those days nonconformism was very popular and some of the Liverpool families found the lifestyle somewhat austere. However many evacuees accompanied their host families to church or chapel and took part in Sunday school and eisteddfods in church or school.

Charlie Green and his brother, **Albert**, *became fully integrated into the Welsh community. "My mum's family were Welsh and, when the bombing started, she sent us, as private evacuees to her relatives. I was sent, aged 5, to my mother's uncle and aunt in Dinorwic. They were quite elderly and very good to me. I stayed for 5 years and soon learned Welsh, which I still like to speak when I get a chance. My younger brother, Albert, followed when he was 3½ and stayed nearby with my mother's cousin and her husband, who was a quarry worker at Dinorwic slate quarry. We went to church regularly and I even won a prayer-book in one Gwyl for my Welsh recitation. I really enjoyed my time in North Wales and don't remember being sad at all."*

Charlie Green's prayer book

Courtesy Charlie Green

Laurence Lloyd recalls: *"I attended morning service with the family, Sunday school in the afternoon and the evening service when the evacuees were expected to recite some scripture in Welsh, which was a good challenge!"*

Dilys Williams recalls: *"Many of the evacuees would come to chapel and some even learned to say their Bible verses in Welsh. They also shared the school with us - the Welsh children were taught in the morning and the English in the afternoon, swapping every other day."*

The May Blitz and second wave of evacuation

The first mass evacuation did not last long for many children and mothers. Over 60% of evacuees had returned to Liverpool by January 1940. Many had found it difficult to settle and suffered from homesickness. Town and country life were hugely different and, whilst many children adapted, some young mothers found it particularly hard to adjust. Clashes of religion and culture were sometimes a problem, especially where Catholic families were billeted with nonconformist Welsh families in relatively remote areas. There was no church for them and less entertainment as there were fewer cinemas or fish and chip shops and no Sunday opening of pubs! The pull of returning home for Christmas was huge and the anticipated air raids hadn't actually happened so the risk of being bombed seemed less acute. During the early part of 1940 many of the Liverpool schools reopened, complete with air raid shelters, so the numbers returning to Liverpool grew even further. As a result, most of those who had been evacuated so promptly at the outbreak of war were back in Liverpool when the bombing began in earnest!

Bombing of Merseyside began in August 1940, with particularly severe raids in December. In February 1941, Hitler sent a directive to his forces ordering them to intensify the bombing, targeting English ports and industrial areas to restrict imports and prevent the manufacture of weapons and other war equipment. Bombing reached a peak in May 1941, known as the May Blitz, when there were 8 nights of successive bombing! Overall Merseyside was the second most bombed area outside of London and the final death toll was twice that of any other port in Britain. Air raid civilian casualties for Liverpool, Bootle, Birkenhead and Wallasey numbered nearly 4,000 dead and 3,812 seriously injured. Over 10,840 houses

Old Edge Hill College, Durning Road, Liverpool

Courtesy of Liverpool Record Office, Liverpool Libraries

were destroyed and 184,295 damaged. Dock buildings, offices, pubs, shops, cinemas, schools, railways and even churches sustained serious damage. The most intense bombing focused on Bootle, that included the northern docks and important shipping lanes, where over nine-tenths of its houses were damaged.

The onset of bombing resulted in a steady trickle of evacuees returning to Wales from December to May but, following the horrors of the May Blitz, this turned into a mass exodus. Some rural Welsh towns and villages were almost overrun with city children. Even those who had been desperately homesick during the first evacuation went back more willingly, with the experience of the air raids and the devastation they caused fresh in their minds.

13th March 1941

During last night's raid windows in every class except one were broken. An incendiary shell pierced the roof of the hall and burned on the floor until extinguished. 29 boys and 24 girls turned up for school but were dismissed until tomorrow.

4th April 1, 1941

11 evacuees left

(NB many more groups of children were steadily evacuated each week after that)

Extract from Bidston Avenue Primary school log-book

Courtesy of Birkenhead Record Office

Bomb damage on Cook Street and the Arcade as seen from Union Court

Courtesy of Liverpool Record Office, Liverpool Libraries

The log-books from the evacuated schools give a good picture of the movement of evacuees in and out of Merseyside as the war progressed. For example, Bidston Avenue Primary School, in Birkenhead, had been evacuated to Hope, near Wrexham, at the beginning of the war but some pupils had returned early in 1940 as the school was re-opened, first on a voluntary basis and later on a shift system. It re-opened, complete with air raid shelter on 1st April 1940. However, by spring 1941, the bombing had begun in earnest and Birkenhead was a key target because of its docks and Cammell Laird Shipyard (see log-book entry).

Sylvia Fairfield was only 3 when her family home in Birkenhead received a direct hit. "My mum, baby sister and I survived as we were in the brick shelter in the garden. I don't really remember much about the bombing but have been terrified of thunder and lightning to this day!"

When the May Blitz started Sheila Williams remembers the whole family hastily leaving their home in Edge Hill to travel to Mold to escape the heavy bombing. "I was only 7 at the time but will always remember that Sunday morning when we walked through town to Central Station, carrying our belongings. We walked down the side of Lewis's as it was still burning and there were fires and smoke everywhere.

We took the train to Birkenhead and then got a bus to Mold, intending to get another bus to Pantymwyn where my uncle had a smallholding. Unfortunately it was late Sunday afternoon when we arrived and there were no more buses. Eventually the billeting officer came and opened up a church hall for us to sleep in. My father went with some other men driving round farms to collect straw to fill the mattresses for us to sleep on. More families arrived on Monday and the WRVS and others rallied round setting up the hall as a rest centre. We were later moved to an old two-roomed hut on Bailey Hill. My aunt and her children had one room and our family – mum, dad, my 3 brothers, me and my little sister - had the other room."

After the war

It was very strange for the evacuees returning to bombed out Liverpool after the rural peace of North Wales. Whole streets had been bombed flat, transport was difficult and sometimes the water supply was restricted. Many experienced mixed emotions, pleased to be back with their families but missing the countryside and the friends they had made in North Wales.

Several evacuees suffered from teasing and even severe bullying when they returned to Merseyside after the war, because of their Welshness!

Charlie Green recalls: "My brother, Albert and I came back to Bootle in 1944 when I was 10 and Albert was 8. We cried our eyes out on the journey home as we were so sad leaving our relatives in Dinorwic where we'd stayed for 5 years. The bus dropped us at St Matthew's Hall and one of my sisters recognised us. Albert couldn't understand English but fortunately I still could, so interpreted for him! Albert was horribly bullied in school, taunted and called, 'Welsh pig'. He had to have lots of fights to survive. Luckily he had a teacher, Miss Williams from Pwllheli, who was kind to him and taught him English again, although that made him the teacher's pet in the eyes of the bullies. She taught him well though, as he got into Bootle Grammar and got a good job later."

Harry Moffitt stayed in Wales for 10 years and might have remained permanently if his family hadn't come to fetch him home! "When I was almost 16, my father and brother came to Pentre Celyn to take me home to Walton,

Liverpool. I found it hard to leave the farm and the family who had looked after me so well. It felt great to be back in Liverpool with my family but it was difficult to adjust to such a different lifestyle. I was only 5 when I was evacuated so didn't really remember Liverpool after 10 years in Wales! I was mocked for my Welsh accent and nicknamed 'Dai bach' at Camell Laird's where I became an apprentice welder! It took me some time to lose the accent."

Alick Stark *spent 7 years near Mold, evacuated initially with Roscoe Primary School from West Derby, and later with his mother and aunt who rented a cottage near Gwernaffield. "I went to a Welsh primary school at first and then onto grammar school in Mold. I loved living in Wales and it broke my heart when we had to go back to Liverpool, but dad was working there so we had no choice."*

Most of the evacuees had experienced a completely different environment and way of life. Their experiences undoubtedly had a lasting impact on them and for many it was the starting point for a lasting enjoyment of and appreciation of the natural world and a deep love for North Wales. Later chapters recount the stories of many of those who kept up their links with North Wales and their host families.

Colomendy National Camp

In addition to the large-scale school and private evacuation described in this chapter, hundreds of Liverpool schoolchildren were evacuated to Colomendy, near Mold, one of the government's purpose-built National Camps. However, the Colomendy story continued long after evacuation and it has played a huge part in developing and strengthening the links between Liverpool and Loggerheads, so the story is told more fully in the next chapter.

Reference: A Welcome in the Hillsides? Jill Wallis; Avid Publications Ltd, 2000

Colomendy School, 'A little bit of Liverpool in North Wales'

Chapter 5

No book on the links between Liverpool and North East Wales would be complete without a chapter about Colomendy, the residential school near Loggerheads that was managed by Liverpool Education Authority for over 65 years. Generations of Liverpool schoolchildren have stayed at Colomendy since it was first built to house evacuees during the Second World War. Over 350,000 pupils have stayed for a week or 2 at the Colomendy Environmental Studies Centre and 6,375 stayed for longer periods at the boarding school.

Colomendy National Camp for evacuees

In 1938, when war was imminent, the government made plans to build a number of residential camps for evacuees to supplement the evacuation to private billets, described in the preceding chapter. The National Camps Corporation was formed to run the camps, whilst the teaching of pupils at the camps remained the responsibility of the education authority from the evacuated area.

Colomendy Hall, near Loggerheads was considered to be an ideal location for a camp and the estate was bought by compulsory purchase in 1939. Two wooden camps were built, each able to house 290 children. The one on the hillside behind the hall became known as Top Camp, and the other on the lower ground below the hall became known as Bottom Camp. They were ready for occupation from spring 1940, and offered to Liverpool Local Education Authority. The bombing of Liverpool was just beginning and many parents were keen for their children to be evacuated.

In April 1940, Dingle Girls' and Boys' Secondary Schools arrived, along with many of their teachers. Dingle was a prime target for bombing as it is situated close to the main dock area and it was also close to an important oil storage depot. Gradually pupils from other schools joined them, including some infant and junior pupils. Many of those who stayed in the early days have memories of limited food, the austere regime and strict discipline.

Edna McCumiskey was one of the first to arrive from Dingle with her younger brother. "I was 12 and stayed for 2 years, until I reached the school leaving age and had to go back to get a job. I didn't enjoy my time at Colomendy and was keen to get home. I was very homesick. It was very bare then, no flower beds, and very cold and basic. We could hear the bombers going overhead each night and watched Liverpool being bombed – the city just glowed every night! We all worried that our parents had been killed.

LIVERPOOL DAILY POST. FRIDAY. MARCH 7. 1941

A CAMPING SCHOOL

LIVERPOOL'S NEW LUNG

The Colomendy School Camp, near Loggerheads, where hundreds of Liverpool schoolchildren evacuated from danger zones in the city have been sojourning since April of last year, is now well out of the experimental stage and important practical results have begun to emerge.

The camp site, set in a fold of the pine-clad hills just beyond Mold, has never been questioned. Parents and children alike have agreed with the authorities, both local and national, that there could scarcely be a more attractive spot upon which to pitch a camp of any kind. The buildings, too, with schoolrooms, dormitories, assembly and dining halls of Canadian cedar and acacia woods; the modern kitchen conveniences and the use of constant hot water and electricity as handmaidens to a standard of scrupulous cleanliness, have taken the eye from the first. Not a mother has grumbled at the comfort or the conditions of life at the camp schools.

Health And Strength

The question has been always whether the children like it; what reaction there has been in body and mind to the novelty and discipline of a "backwood" existence on communal

The official ans' statistical grs and wei'

...rl pupils in the Domestic Science class at the ...ndy School camp. Bottom: A warm meal provid... for new arrivals in the dining-room.

What I most remember is the food – very little and not very good. I had one egg in 2 years! They cooked them all in big trays and sliced them up! We each had a yolk one day and the white the next! We were always hungry and used to buy any food that was available at Cadole shop - carrots, oxo cubes - anything! We picked whinberries and anything else we could find to put between our bread. I still can't waste any food today and don't understand how people can throw so much away!"

Many of the evacuees remember a poem about the food. It was usually sung to the tune of 'There is a happy land far, far away'.

"There's a horrid camp far, far away
Where we have bread and jam three times a day
Egg and bacon we never see
Sugar is as scarce as tea
And we are gradually fading away!"

Some of the boys quoted another version:

"There is a Nazi* camp far, far away
Where we had bread and jam three times a day
Egg and bacon we didn't see
Dirty big beetles in our tea
That's why we are gradually fading away!"

*The camp was known as Colomendy NCC, standing for National Camps Corporation but the lads renamed it Nazi concentration camp!

Marjorie Jones was evacuated to Colomendy for 5 months when she was 12. "We went to the dining room for our evening meal which was usually bread and margarine, known as bread and scrape, and cold lumpy custard. I was glad to go home!"

Lynn Milburn was evacuated with her brothers from West Derby after the bombing started. "In a way we were lucky as we arrived at a purpose-built camp that had been erected specially for Liverpool children, but I felt awful. I had this terrible feeling or pain, or both, in the pit of my tummy, I just sat on the steps of my dormitory and wanted to cry (but didn't)."

Peter McGlone was evacuated after the May Blitz from Norris Green, aged 7, and stayed for 7 years. "We were all given jobs and once a week we put our own underwear in a bag and had to wash them – sometimes things got muddled but you had to wash them whether they were yours or not!"

Billy Ingham, who was evacuated from Everton Valley in 1940, recalls: "You had to be up at 7:00am in the morning and had to strip to your underpants to go and get washed - it was really cold! If there were ever any difficulties between the boys it would be settled with the boxing gloves on outside the dorms. Each dorm had a gang and one weekend we played Robin Hood in the woods, making wooden lances with pocket-knives. I got knocked in the face and part of my tooth broke. There was lots of blood and the games were stopped!"

With time, most children settled in and came to love the outdoor life. Lessons were usually held in the mornings and afternoons were free for exploring. Everyone remembers climbing up Moel Famau or the steep Cat Walk at Loggerheads.

Violet Paton was evacuated with her sister Lily and her 4 brothers from Edge Hill, Liverpool. "Initially, I was very homesick and didn't like the dormitories and bunk-beds or hearing the German planes flying over on their way to Liverpool. However, I loved the environment and nature, being able to go walking around Loggerheads and Moel Famau, picking bilberries and eating them raw, finding wild strawberries and hazelnuts. I loved the opportunities for sport: running races, rounders with the other girls, cricket with the boys and sliding on the ice in the winter."

Jean Burslem, who was evacuated from Everton in 1940, has happy memories of the year she spent at Colomendy. "I loved the outdoor activities *and it triggered a lasting love for the countryside. I remember picking fruit – blackberries and bilberries – which was wonderful for a child from the city."*

Lynn Milburn *recalls: "School was in the morning and afternoons were spent on rambles around the countryside, up and down the surrounding hills – something I have enjoyed doing ever since."*

Edna McCumiskey *recalls: "We walked up Moel Famau regularly, always walking in long lines. We wore our shoes out within weeks so then we got boots but they wore out too so finally we had clogs that never wore out!"*

Billy Ingham *recalls: "I remember Moel Famau well as we went to the top many times and would play hide and seek in the bracken. I also enjoyed walking along the Leete and swimming in the deeper parts of the river."*

However, many of the youngsters were acutely homesick and were desperately worried about their families during the bombing. Many tried to run away, with some making repeated escapes. Local police, and bus drivers were used to handling the situation and usually the escapees were returned to Colomendy quickly, where they often received harsh punishment.

Moel Famau from the Leete Path

Courtesy of the Morris Family

Peter McGlone *loved Colomendy but remembers the unhappiness of many other lads. "Lots of lads couldn't stand it and did a bunk but were usually caught before they got to Mold and brought back. 4 of us more established ones used to try and sort out any problems, usually homesickness, and encourage the lads to stay."*

Lynn Milburn*, who came to Colomendy when she was 13, recalls: "At first our parents visited once a month but, after a few months, they stopped coming. We weren't given a reason so I invented my own, which gave me nightmares as there were rumours that Liverpool had been bombed flat! I hatched a plan to run away. I didn't tell anybody, not even my brothers, and saved up 7d (old money). On the next afternoon walk I made sure I was near the back, then pretended to bend down and tie my shoe-laces. As soon as they had gone round the next bend I scooted off in the other direction. I walked about 3 miles to the nearest town, inside hedges so I wouldn't be caught, and caught a bus to Birkenhead.*

I didn't know how far 7d would get me and didn't want to draw attention to myself so, after some time, I got off the bus but was still a long way from Birkenhead. I decided to try and thumb a lift and, luckily, the car that stopped was going through the tunnel to Liverpool. The gentleman driving was obviously very worried about me and I think he guessed what was happening as runaway evacuees were quite common. Reluctantly he dropped me at the Liverpool end of the tunnel as he was going in the opposite direction to my home in West Derby. I was dismayed to discover that all the trams had stopped running due to the bombing and I was faced with another 6 or 7 mile walk home! As I walked up our road the first person I saw was my little sister swinging on the gate. The look of shock on her face! She didn't say anything but ran to tell my parents who didn't believe her. I was put straight to bed, which I was glad of. I wasn't sent back to Colomendy and my brothers came home at the end of the next term."

Billy Ingham and 3 friends escaped in winter. "We planned our escape for 4 to 5 weeks beforehand. Whenever we got cake or food we kept it. On the night of our escape we put things in our beds to look like we were still there so the staff didn't notice we had gone. We left at 4am when everyone was asleep. There was thick snow, it was cold and our feet were wet. On the way we pinched cabbages and turnips from farmers' fields and ate them. We got to Chester by morning, intending to get the bus, but didn't have enough money. We asked someone for help and they took us to the police station. By now we were freezing cold and soaking wet and it was still snowing. The police rang our parents and the school who sent a vehicle with snow chains on to take us back to Colomendy. The teachers had reassured our parents that they would put us to bed and look after us, as they worried we had caught a chill. However, we were in deep trouble and got 'six of the best' the next morning. When our parents found out about this punishment, they brought us home.

Wendy Carroll, who was evacuated from Aigburth when she was only 6 or 7, tried to escape three times! "The first time we only got as far as Mold. We were better prepared for our second attempt and had even held a concert in the air raid shelter to raise money for food and bus fare! That time we made it home but my dad took us back the next morning. On the third occasion we got back to my friend's house in Wavertree but were returned to Colomendy once again."

Wendy and her cousin Norma at Colomendy

Courtesy of Wendy Carroll

Post-war Colomendy – the lung for Liverpool

After the war, Colomendy continued to be used by Liverpool LEA for children who would benefit from a boarding school education. Some were sent on medical grounds because they were frail or recovering from illness and it was hoped that the countryside environment and nutritious food would reap health benefits. Others were sent if there were domestic problems such as parental illness, overcrowding in the home, or financial hardship. The bombing had destroyed hundreds of homes so many families were living in exceptionally cramped conditions. Other families were struggling to make ends meet as so many fathers had been killed in the war or had returned home injured and unable to work. It was also felt that the experience of community living would be valuable for the children in later life.

Inspector's report 1958: "Colomendy has been of very real benefit to many thousands of Liverpool children who would otherwise have had little opportunity to enjoy the benefits of an open air life in really beautiful surroundings."

There was always an outdoor focus to the teaching with numerous walks where pupils were taught about the local geography and wildlife, learning to appreciate the countryside, understand animal signs and recognise the season changes. Most of the pupils who came to board during the 1950s and early 1960s have very happy memories, both of the school itself and the surrounding area, and loved the fresh air and freedom.

Mike MacKenzie from Old Swan stayed from 1957 to 1962. "Like most of the pupils I was homesick the first term but the penny dropped in the second term and I started to enjoy myself. The walks and wonderful surroundings awakened me to the natural world and took my blinkers off. The teachers broadened my horizons, introducing me to classical music, cricket and the environment. I consider myself very privileged to have gone there."

Donald McCowen was sent to stay at Colomendy in 1956, aged 12, for health reasons, to get away from the city into the country air. "I came initially for 3 months but, when I got home asked if I could go back and stayed for another 3 years, becoming head boy! My best time of the week was the 2 hours free time after the religious service on Sunday, which I spent walking along the Leete at Loggerheads or up onto the Cat Walk to the top of the cliff."

Rita Sharp came to stay in 1956. "I was the seventh of 10 children living in our terraced house in Aigburth. My dad had cancer so it was really hard for my mum to manage with us all at home. Mum had heard that Colomendy

Netball team, 1956 (Rita is on the front left)

Courtesy of Colomendy Connection Archive

was a boarding school for Liverpool children whose families were having difficulties coping due to illness, bereavement etc and wondered whether any of my brothers would be able to go. I went with my mum to a meeting about Colomendy where the lady explained that there were no places available for boys at that time but asked if I would like to go instead as there was room for a girl. I immediately said, 'yes', and went soon after when I was 13. I stayed for 2 years and absolutely loved it. I have lots of happy memories of Colomendy and the surrounding area."

During the war years, the school had grown food as part of the 'Dig for Victory' campaign and, after the war, pupils continued to tend the gardens, growing fruit and vegetables and keeping poultry. From 1949, Rural Studies became an increasingly important part of the curriculum and a proper working farm was also established at the school from 1956. The older boys were used as stockmen, feeding the animals and doing the day to day maintenance. By the late 1950s, girls also were allowed to help on the farm and stockyard. This work was very popular and some pupils even stayed in the holidays to look after the livestock. It triggered a lasting interest for many and several boys took agricultural apprenticeships after leaving Colomendy and later worked on farms. One such ex-

Skiffle Group, 1958

Courtesy of Colomendy Connection Archive

Digging up the land behind the assembly room circa late 1940s/ early 1950s

Courtesy of Colomendy Connection Archive

On the farm circa 1960s

Courtesy of Colomendy Connection Archive

pupil, John Grogan, even joined the staff, becoming farm manager in 1965.

Donald McCowen recalls: "I enjoyed looking after the pigs. I remember helping, late at night, when one sow was having her litter. One of the piglets was weak and had to be helped out. I stayed on in the holidays to look after the animals and lived in the White House, the Headmaster's House, where I loved the cook's delicious meals!"

Norman Nickson and Mr Kane with the combine harvester (Why does Norman look like he's Lord of the Manor?)

Courtesy of Colomendy Connection Archive

Ron Sinclair recalls: "Mr Kane, who established the farm, was an inspiration to all the children who worked on the farm. Many like me went on to farm schools."

Sally Hesketh enjoyed being a stockgirl in the early 1960s. "Sometimes lessons would be interrupted by Miss Bryan (the stock manager) who would pull us out to tend to the animals. We always welcomed the chance!"

George Andrews, who stayed at Colomendy from 1953-54, recalls, "I spent most of my time in the stockyard looking after the chickens, guinea fowl, geese and ducks. I didn't realise that guinea fowl could fly and, one evening when I was trying to get them back into the shed quickly, they ran down the field and took off into the trees, so I had to leave them out overnight. I shut the shed door and told the teachers I'd put them away! I left grain out in the pen and was relieved to find them all there the next morning. I'd have been in trouble if they hadn't been!"

Glan Alyn Boarding School

The original wooden camps were in need of refurbishment by the 1960s and were not considered to be suitable for a permanent boarding school. A new purpose-built boarding school, named Glan Alyn was begun in 1967 and

Dancing on the raised lawn circa 1957

Courtesy of Colomendy Connection Archive

opened in 1969. The Top Camp facilities were also upgraded and it became the centre for Visiting School Groups. Glan Alyn had places for 150 pupils and aimed to offer secondary education up to sixteen for Liverpool pupils who would benefit from a boarding school education. Unfortunately it became increasingly difficult to recruit pupils and the boarding school was closed in 1990, after which the buildings became part of the Environmental Education Centre for Visiting Schools.

Darryl Gregson and his brother *Haydn* stayed at Glan Alyn in the 1970s for 7 or 8 years. Darryl remembers: "We lived in Broad Green with our mum as, like so many of our friends, our parents had divorced. Mum showed me a

Haydn Gregson at Glan Alyn

Courtesy of Darryl Gregson

106

*brochure about Colomendy and asked if I would like to go there. I liked the look
of the outdoor stuff on offer – camping, canoeing, rock-climbing – so I said,
'yes'. My brother joined me later, along with some of our other friends from
Broad Green. I really enjoyed living there – it was one of the happiest times of
my life. I now own more climbing and sailing equipment than you can imagine
and spend as much of my spare time following my outdoor interests."*

Colomendy Visiting School

In addition to the pupils who boarded, a wide variety of groups visited Colomendy
for shorter periods, either for holidays in the country or for a more structured
programme of study. For many of the city children. It was their first experience
of the natural world and their first holiday without their parents.

***Hilda Murray** went on a trip to Colomendy with her school in the late
1940s. "My mum had to save 15 shillings for each of us to send me and my
two sisters. We didn't have a suitcase so had to use a pillowcase. It was our
first holiday."*

***Joyce Boyd** stayed at Colomendy for a week in both 1946 and 1947. She
was given a free place the first time as her dad had lost a leg during the war*

and could not work. "We had lessons every morning in the classroom, but the afternoons were spent out doing nature studies, collecting flowers and pressing them, climbing Moel Famau and we even went into the caves at Loggerheads. From then on I was always into nature."

David Backhouse commented: "Ask any kid brought up in Liverpool in the 1950s what their best holiday was and the answer would be 'Colomendy'!"

In the 1950s, teacher **Beryl Hughes (neé Smith)** brought her pupils from West Derby to Colomendy for an annual fortnight's stay. "The visit gave them a real love of the countryside. I was so impressed with Colomendy that I later applied for a full-time job and taught there for 3 years. I loved the place and the opportunities it gave the children."

Gordon Davies remembers, "I went there from Anfield Road Junior School in 1955 or 1956 when I was 9 or 10. It was the first time I had had a holiday and, coming from a small terraced house in Liverpool, it was quite a culture shock. I think it cost £10, which was a lot of money to scrimp and save in those days. I can remember the hut we slept in and the bunk-beds quite well and I recall a long hike up a steep hill, which must have been Moel Famau. In those

Milking at Cae'r Odyn Farm

Courtesy of Colomendy Museum

Quarry visit by
Broad Square
Primary School,
1990

Courtsey of Ann Butler

days there were no walking boots or cagoules, just your everyday shoes, a gaberdine raincoat and canvas haversack. The last evening, we had a singsong around the camp fire and we thought it was fantastic."

Gordon Jones *first came to Colomendy as a 10 year old with Sudley Primary School. "I still remember the sense of adventure we all had as we boarded the bus and set off through the tunnel, through the Wirral and into Wales. Once we had crossed the blue bridge over the River Dee and started to climb Ewloe Hill, we were in the countryside. We had lessons every morning to do with the day's activities eg before a walk up Moel Famau we learnt about contour lines and very basic map reading. Each day we had to keep a diary of all our activities. I think we were given 'I Spy the Countryside' books in which to record all the new objects and wildlife we encountered. For most of us, this was our first significant time away from home without our parents and, for me, as an only child, my first experience of community living. I thoroughly enjoyed my time there."*

Colomendy Environmental Studies Centre

Liverpool Corporation bought Colomendy when the National Camps wound up in 1957. The Visiting School was given greater emphasis with the appointment of a dedicated Warden in 1958, who increased the environmental and rural studies activities offered. As well as a general introduction to the countryside, geography, nature study, geology and local history were taught. Visits were made to local farms, quarries, hillforts, historic houses, local villages and market towns. Later a series of Nature Trails were developed in the grounds and a bird hide built.

> **Tony Jones** *from Cae'r Odyn Farm, Tafarn-y-Gelyn, enjoyed taking visiting groups around his farm. "For most of the youngsters it was the first time they had seen a cow close up and some didn't realise that was where we got our milk from!"*

The number of secondary groups visiting increased during the 1960s when fieldwork became an important part of the curriculum in biology, geology, geography and history. A trip to Colomendy was an ideal way for city teachers to deliver the coursework element of CSE geography, as pupils had to produce a folder of fieldwork. Visits to Colomendy remained relevant when the National Curriculum and the GCSE exam were introduced in the 1980s. During the 1970s and 80s, over 10,000 children per year came to stay at Colomendy for a week of environmental studies and outdoor education. In addition, it was used for teacher training and by a variety of youth groups. It was probably the largest centre of its kind in the country, providing for a wide range of ages, from 5-18 and beyond.

*Teacher **Christine Mason** brought 12 and 13 year olds from Notre Dame High School, Woolton, in the 70s. "They were good experiences because it was the first time many children had been away from home. They were excited at nights and the dormitories were busy with midnight feasts etc! History, geography and maths teachers accompanied the groups and we had lessons, such as studying the River Alyn, measuring the rate of flow, taking water samples, as well as lots of great walks."*

***Alec Butler** brought groups from 2 Liverpool Special Schools in the 1980s and 90s. "The River Alyn ran through the grounds and they loved pond-dipping with nets. I'd get them to collect materials in the woods to make mini-rafts that we raced down the river. We'd always walk up Moel Famau, kidding the children that there was a café on the top, to encourage them up the hill! The older pupils would do more adventurous activities like gorge walking, rock-climbing and abseiling. It was a fantastic experience for them all.*

*My late wife, **Ann Butler**, probably came to Colomendy more than any other teacher. She brought special needs and mainstream classes from Broad Square County Primary School in Norris Green for over 30 years! Working with children was her whole life and Colomendy provided the ideal environment in which to do it – she felt her pupils benefited enormously from their stays at Colomendy."*

***Erin Durrant** spent a week at Colomendy with Phoenix School, Edge Hill, in 2008, when she was 8. "I liked it when we went fishing in the Alyn. We caught some tadpoles and bullheads but put them back as it's cruel to keep fish out of water. We walked to the Leete and did some nature spotting and saw some squirrels and bluetits. It was lovely waking in the morning and seeing the rabbits and squirrels playing on the grass. I loved being in the countryside – it's so different from being in the city."*

Colomendy Centre for Education and Adventure

Colomendy is still owned by Liverpool City Council but is now operated by outdoor education provider, Kingswood. A major refurbishment in 2006, funded by the Big Lottery and Liverpool City Council, included building a caving facility, a lake for watersports and high ropes courses as well as upgrading the accommodation. Colomendy is now a flagship Educational Activity Centre, attracting groups from across Britain and Europe. Liverpool LEA have retained strong links with the centre and Liverpool schools are given priority for bookings, ensuring that Liverpool schoolchildren continue to benefit from visits to Colomendy.

Colomendy visits by Broad Square Primary School, 1988, 1989, 1990

Courtsey of Ann Butler

Expeditions and
adventures

In many ways, teenagers growing up in the 1940s, 50s and 60s had far more freedom than today's youngsters. Traffic is so much heavier and faster, so it's not as easy to cycle to and fro, and parental concerns for children's safety seem greater. Modern youngsters are often absorbed with a surfeit of electronic entertainment or seem under pressure to do a multitude of organised activities, so they lack the motivation, time or opportunity to explore and find the outdoor adventure that their predecessors revelled in.

Jackie Robertson sums it up: "In the 1950s we were lucky to be able to cycle anywhere on our own, or youth hostel or camp in safety, with our parents' blessing. We used to go to the baths on our own, or Guides, or shopping, or dancing, without the necessary parental supervision expected nowadays in these troubled times."

Hundreds of Merseyside youngsters got their first taste of freedom and experience of the countryside on trips to North Wales organised by numerous youth groups in Liverpool, including Scouts, Guides, youth clubs and Boys' Brigades. Without these organised groups, few youngsters would have had the opportunity or the confidence to explore the countryside. For many it was an experience that triggered a lasting love of the outdoors and an interest in the environment. The youth leaders lit the touch paper and fanned the flames of interest, and the landscape of the Clwydian Range did the rest!

Roy Shiel camping with the Scouts

Courtesy of Jean Shiel

David Shiel remembers: "My dad came to this area for the first time with the Scouts. He used to say for a young lad growing up in the 1950s, joining the scouts was the easiest way to get out of the city and get a taste of the countryside."

Reg Fletcher recalls how he and a gang of boys cycled regularly all the way to Loggerheads in the 1930s when he was about 16 with Albion House Club (which started in 1932 and is still a thriving youth club today): "We would go Friday evening, stay Saturday and leave on Sunday, camping on the rock at the top of Loggerheads and visiting Maeshafn and Moel Famau. We would sit in the evenings

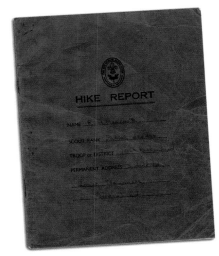

Hike report

Courtesy of Ronnie Meacock

playing the guitar and accordion, having a good time, but not causing any trouble!"

Bob Griffiths, *originally from Tranmere but now living in North Wales, was a member of the 10th Birkenhead Scout troop in the 1950s. "As a young boy of 14, living in a town, it was through the membership of a large and successful Scout group, that I developed a fascination for the countryside. My scouting pals and I took every opportunity to take a bus from Birkenhead to Mold or Loggerheads and, with a rucksack, sleeping bag, hike tent and map, would venture off into the hills in the Ruthin area, camping overnight in fields, with the permission of the friendly farmers. In those days there weren't the restrictions there are now – we didn't have a leader with us, and were just given map references and left to complete 15 miles in two days!*

I remember an expedition to Moel Famau in 1958. We walked all day around the hills and villages of the Loggerheads area and camped in a farmer's field. We cooked ourselves liver, gravy, peas and potatoes and slept out in the open, despite being offered the barn by the farmer. The next day, after walking to

Cub-scouts hiking

Courtesy of Bob Griffiths

Cub-scout camp at
Bacheriog

Courtesy of Bob Griffiths

the top of Moel Famau, we missed the last bus from Loggerheads and had to walk to Mold to get the next one to Birkenhead – being Scouts of course we got back safely!"

Tony Roberts also has wonderful memories of his Scout expeditions. "I was a member of the 32nd Chester Scout troop and, in the early 1950s we would, quite frequently, get the bus to Mold and then take a hard day's walk through Loggerheads and on up to the top of Moel Famau. In the late 1950s and early 60s, it was quite normal for a number of us, as Senior Scouts (15 - 18years) and later as Rover Scouts (18 - 25years), after a social evening in the Scout HQ, to catch the last bus to Mold and then do a night-hike to the top of Moel Famau and then along the Clwydian Range to Bodfari to catch the bus home next morning!!"

Colin Legg had been evacuated to the area but later returned with the scouts whilst a pupil at Liverpool Institute. He recalls his scout expedition: "We did an overnight hike for our First Class Journey on Moel Famau and it poured all night. My guardian was quite worried about me and yet had never been concerned when I was out in Liverpool!"

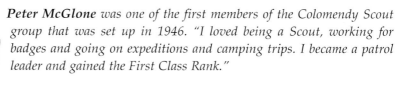

Peter McGlone was one of the first members of the Colomendy Scout group that was set up in 1946. "I loved being a Scout, working for badges and going on expeditions and camping trips. I became a patrol leader and gained the First Class Rank."

Maidie Brown was introduced to the area as a Guide. "I came in 1940-41 as a member of the Guide company from Wirral Grammar School for Girls. I loved the Guide camps at Cilcain and remember 5 of us having an overnight on the slopes of Moel Famau and dragging up a heavy trek cart of gear! I later came back as a Ranger Guide, staying at Maeshafn Youth Hostel. These early visits gave me a lasting love for the area and the outdoors."

Albert and *Charlie Green* were introduced to Moel Famau and Denbighshire as teenagers through trips with the Boys' Brigade. Both later became leaders and brought many young Liverpool lads on expeditions to the area, sharing their love for the outdoors and this part of North Wales. Charlie recalls: "As a teenager I was a keen member of the Boys' Brigade at St Leonard's, Bootle and loved going on seasonal expeditions to Moel Famau. We used to get the bus to Loggerheads then walk up Moel Famau. We often cycled to Loggerheads too, initially through the Boys' Brigade but later on our own. A group of 6 of us went down one of the potholes - scrambling down the rock face and then into the cave and along the pothole tunnel as far as we could go!

As an adult in the 1960s I became a Boys' Brigade leader and took groups to camp in Cilcain or stay at Plas Drâw, Llangynhafal, sleeping in a barn. The boys trained for and undertook their Duke of Edinburgh expeditions on the Clwydian Hills. My brother Albert also became a leader in Bootle and used to bring groups to Cyffylliog and Bontuchel, staying in the village hall, or youth hostel."

Scout badges

Courtesy of Peter McGlone

Boys' Brigade Group on Moel Famau, in the 1960s

Courtesy of Charlie Green

Many other youngsters arranged their own trips, but these were often triggered by earlier experiences as Guides, Scouts or with other youth groups. Their introduction to hiking, camping through the organised groups gave them the confidence and motivation to explore independently and build on their earlier experiences.

The Caravan Crew

During the 1950s, a group of young people from Bebington on the Wirral, from their mid-teens to early twenties, regularly came to stay in a simple wooden gypsy caravan at Bryn Bowlio Farm, Llanferres. The founder members were all Ranger Guides but the group became much wider, as brothers, friends and other like-minded individuals joined them, sometimes spilling over into another caravan nearby. They used to catch the bus to Loggerheads or Mold and then walk to the caravan, occasionally they'd cycle over or, in later years, some would hitch-hike (safe to do in the early 1950s).

Gradually, as they moved away from the area for study, work or marriage, the group dwindled and eventually the visits came to an end, but the happy times they spent there remain with them all. Their evocative log-books tell the story of the carefree, happy times they spent in the foothills of Moel Famau. They revelled in the freedom and loved to explore the area. It gave them all a lasting love of the countryside.

Log-book entries

(these were written by several people so no names have been attributed)

The Caulfield caravan at Bryn Bowlio Farm

Courtesy of Mike Bridgewater, photo by Mike Shiel

"The caravan was a cosy place. We sang and made music, did country dancing in the field and talked till all hours. We catered for ourselves using the wood-burning stove and lit oil lamps in the evening. It was wonderful to have such freedom. No one ever wanted to go home."

"We explored all over the valley, by day and night, whenever we could. Our knowledge of the area grew and grew. We had all weathers and all seasons to enjoy, and knew the trees and plantations on the way. We knew where the wild flowers grew, and the berries, wild strawberries, blackberries, bilberries and hazel nuts and field mushrooms in their season."

"There was a valley deep in shadow to our left and to our right, another valley. Here the evening sun shone brightly, showing up every little detail - the bright green of the bogs, the rust of the bracken, the rich, dark colour of the heather, the occasional yellow blaze where a gorse bush was in flower - all the colours intensified by the evening light."

"At the river, we discovered a fairly narrow tree which had blown down and now lay across the river. A lot of time was spent crawling across it and then we started to walk, very slowly across it. Vic nearly came to a bad end, but

*Assorted photos
from the log-books*

Courtesy of Ken Steel

119

The River Alyn

Courtesy of Mike Shiel

cleverly managed to land on dry land, after giving everyone heart failure!"

"We would even go out when the moon was bright, walking up the mountain road to Moel Famau, listening to the owls hooting, and marvelling at the wonderful fireflies that glowed and danced in the hedges of the lanes."

"We found orchids and a lovely crimson sweetbriar rose and more milkwort. Then we climbed up the blinding white limestone path to Eryrys Rocks. Oh, it was hot! The last bit of climbing was awful, but worth the trouble. The view from the top was magnificent. We could see a shepherd on the opposite hillside, herding sheep from one field to another, and the whole panorama of the valley laid out before us. The sun was just the right temperature up there, with a fresh little breeze to lessen the burning of it. There was a smell of warm thyme and sheep. The glaring white rocks were too hot to touch but snails tried to go on them before discovering their mistake. We dozed, ate Spangles and felt we were in paradise."

"We reached the top of the mountain (Moel Famau) ten minutes after the sun had set. We sat and watched the evening star. The sky was a mass of red clouds

Looking from Eryrys Rocks

Courtesy of the 'caravan crew'

and the view was perfect. It was too cold to stay on top of the tower, so we found a cosy spot in the heather, out of the wind and put on all our warm jerseys, macs, scarves, and gloves, as a few bats flitted about. Then we settled down to eat a snack and silence fell. We sat companionably watching as lights came on in all the valleys, and red lights in Wirral across the Dee. Vehicles headlights flashed in the sky as they breasted a hill. We could also see lights all over Merseyside."

On top of Moel Famau

Courtesy of Mike Shiel

In about 1952, Steve Macfarlane, a young architect who lived in a small bothy at Bryn Bowlio, drew up plans for a Village Hall in Llanferres. This was to be built by volunteers from the local community assisted by young people from across Europe (members of the International Voluntary Service for Peace). Through Steve, members of the 'caravan crew' met both the local and the international volunteers and regularly joined their work parties.

Jackie Robertson recalls: "We met all sorts of people from foreign parts, and we enjoyed learning their songs and stories around the stove in the caravan

in the evenings after the work was done. It was wonderful to see the village hall gradually taking shape and to feel we'd been a part of it from the beginning."

Vic Mason recalls: "A particularly memorable event of 1956 was the arrival of I.V.S.P. volunteers, during the latter half of July and the first 2 weeks of August, to decorate and paint the hall and level out the surrounding site in preparation for its opening to the public. The international group included several of us 'vanners'."

Working on Llanferres Village Hall

Courtesy of the 'caravan crew'

School visits

Numerous Merseyside schools have used Moel Famau, Loggerheads and the Clwydian Range for field trips, hikes and days out. Several colleges also use the area for the development of teamwork and leadership as well as navigation, rock climbing and abseiling.

The longest standing and most regular visitors must be Kingsmead School in Hoylake. The whole school has been coming for an annual hike up Moel Famau since 1907, and articles in the school magazines suggest that the pupils have always enjoyed it and that the habits of the youngsters haven't significantly changed! In the early days the journey was on a series of steam trains, leaving Great Meols Station, changing at Bidston and

a further change at Hope Exchange to alight finally at Rhydymwyn. They left at 8.00am and didn't get back until 10pm.

The school magazine of 1907 recalls the descent from Moel Famau: "We ran, we jumped, we fell, we dived, we rolled, we slid, we landed painfully in innumerable gorse bushes and at intervals we stood and laughed at the funny sight presented by the others, conscious all the while that as a spectacle we were not a whit behind those at whom we laughed. It was undignified but it was great fun, and it made us more than ready for the tea that was waiting for us at Loggerheads."

Duke of Edinburgh groups

In recent years, the popularity of some of the organised groups like the Boys' Brigade and Guide and Scout movements has waned, as teenage tastes and aspirations have changed. However, the Duke of Edinburgh Award scheme, which was introduced in 1956, to encourage the personal development of young people from all backgrounds, remains popular. Many Merseyside secondary schools and youth groups still run the scheme today. One component is an expedition for which the participants have to learn map-reading, navigation and survival skills. The Clwydian Range is used regularly for the bronze expeditions and silver and gold expedition training. During spring and summer, hundreds of youngsters from Merseyside can still be found, checking maps and carrying heavy rucsacks, on the lanes and footpaths around Moel Famau.

Modern teenagers have a much wider view of the world than their predecessors due to modern media, but it's easy to forget that city teenagers are still unfamiliar with farming and countryside lore as they rarely have the opportunity to have direct experience. One teacher recounted an anecdote about a bright girl who had commented that the sheep's fur was quite scraggy and hadn't realised it was

Public service students from Knowsley Community College

Courtesy of Lorna Jenner

124

wool! It is only by getting out into the countryside that they have the chance to gain familiarity and understanding. Learning to be at ease in the outdoor environment, taking responsibility for your own safety, dealing with bad weather, navigation problems and other difficulties helps to build self-confidence and resilience, as much today as it did a generation ago.

In April 2009, public service students from Knowsley Community College, completed a hike around Moel Famau as part of their training for the silver Duke of Edinburgh expedition, and were enthusiastic about the experience. They had enjoyed being in the hills and were satisfied that they had navigated the route successfully. Only one had been to the area before but many were keen to return.

> ***Kaitlyn Bryrne***, *who had got seriously lost the year before on her Bronze expedition, was really exhilarated by her success this time. "I feel like I'm on top of the world now I've done that! I'll definitely come back here again – I can imagine coming up here with a boyfriend, walking with the dogs, and, if I've got kids of my own in the future, I'd definitely bring them up here."*

> ***Emma Bruffell*** *ended her walk barefoot as her new boots had rubbed. "We got lost, I lost a toe-nail and got blisters, but I still enjoyed myself and would like to come back!"*

> ***Ashley Butcher*** *commented: "The sheep scared me. There was a whole group in front of the gate we had to go through and I didn't like walking past them, as I didn't know whether they were going to run at me! I still enjoyed it though and it was good to work as a team and learn new skills like map-reading. I'd come back here again – it'd be a great place to bring kids."*

> ***Kieran Breen*** *enjoyed being on the summit of Moel Famau, commenting:*

A lasting bond

For many of those Merseysiders who spent time in North East Wales during their childhood and teenage years, the experience has had a lasting mark on their lives. For some it was where they met their future husband or wife, others formed lasting friendships, many return for holidays and visits, others bought caravans or holiday homes and some have even moved to live permanently in North Wales.

Romance and friendship

Many Liverpool girls joined the Land Army as part of the war effort and some were sent to work on farms in North East Wales.

Olwen Jones *came to Mold from Wavertree with the Land Army, just after the war ended in 1947. "I lodged at Bryn Alyn Hostel, Rhydymwyn, and worked mainly at Gwasaney Farm where I was milking. I met my future husband, John Alyn, whilst I was a Land Girl and, when the Land Army finished in 1948, I did not return to Liverpool but married and settled in Mold. Many of the other land girls also married locals and settled in the area."*

Olwen as a Land Girl and on her wedding day

Courtesy of Olwen Jones

Pat returning to Cilcain in summer, 1955

Courtesy of Pat Hartley

*Former evacuee to Cilcain, **Pat Hartley**, met her future husband through the family she had been billeted with: "I kept in touch with the folk from Derwen Cottage and in the early 1950s I drove back to Cilcain to see Auntie Nan. I visited many more times and eventually, in the 1960s, married Auntie Nan's nephew John. I brought my step-children back to Cilcain many times, spending happy holidays staying in a little wooden chalet that John's family owned. I now live nearby in Hawarden as my love of North Wales has never left me."*

***Mary Bartley** lived in the old part of Huyton and, in 1957, when she was 15 she came with her family for her first holiday, staying in a wooden chalet on the Gronfoel Farm, Cilcain. "My uncle's car got stuck in a ditch on the road up to the farm and the farmer sent his son, Ralph, to fetch the tractor to pull us out. During the week's holiday, Ralph 'chatted me up' and we went for walks together when he came home from work. After our holiday Ralph regularly used to come to see me in Huyton, catching the bus from Pantymwyn to Birkenhead, then the ferry and finally the bus to Huyton. Sometimes I did the travelling instead, ending with the bus to Loggerheads and walking to Ralph's sister who lived nearby. We often climbed Moel Famau together and I grew to love the hills. I moved over to Wales when we married in 1966 and we lived in Pantymwyn. We must have started a trend as 2 of Ralph's brothers later married girls from Liverpool themselves! "*

Now we're retired and our children are grown up, we've moved back to Cilcain, where we first met. We still love going out walking with the dog, looking at the flowers and enjoying the views."

Lasting Friendships

Many people talk warmly of the lasting friendships they made, particularly those evacuees who stayed with one family for several years or those who used to holiday regularly at the same place. For many years afterwards youngsters

used to travel between Merseyside and North Wales, to stay with their friends. Whilst the city dwellers enjoyed a stay in the country, the Welsh youngsters equally enjoyed staying in the city, which was often a novel and quite exciting experience.

Ralph and Mary Bartley below Moel Famau near Gronfoel Farm

Courtesy of Lorna Jenner

Dilys Roberts *lived in Llanferres but her father's family were in Liverpool. Almost every weekend a group of relatives came from Liverpool to visit, initially on the Crosville bus, but later by car. "My cousins loved coming to the countryside and they weren't used to seeing cows, sheep and horses. I equally enjoyed going to stay with my aunt in Old Swan, Liverpool. For me, the city was a whole new world. I'd never seen roller skates or toffee apples and it was great to be able to ride a bike on flat pavement or tarmac – not something we could do in Llanferres as my home was at the top of a hill surrounded by fields! I remember being taken down to the docks where they had a pet market and seeing monkeys and other exotic animals in cages as well as puppies and kittens! I was amazed to see a Chinese sailor with a long black plait, hat and tunic – no-one like that came to Llanferres!"*

*The five girls in
the sea at Blundell
Sands*

Courtesy of Rene Smith

*Sisters, Rene Smith, Glenys Edwards
and **Eirlys Lewis**, lived on a hilltop farm
at Tafarn-y-Gelyn, near Loggerheads.
Glenys explains:* "Our farm was a long
walk from the village so we couldn't go
down to the village to play. We loved the
summer holidays when families from
Liverpool used to stay in a caravan
in one of the fields as we had other
children to play with. Two or three
families came regularly and we became
very good friends with their children.
When we were older, we used to go and stay with them in Liverpool for
holidays and, when I went to college in Liverpool, I even lodged with one of
the families."

Rene recalls their early visits to Liverpool: "The journey was very exciting for
us, going on the ferry and the trams. We didn't have electricity on the farm, so
it was a great novelty to switch the lights on and off in the house in Liverpool!
I remember being taken to the seaside for the first time. Our little sister was
a bit scared at first but soon joined us paddling and sitting in the water. We
were envious of our Liverpool friends, Enid and Joan, who could swim!"

***Enid Butler** and her twin sister **Joan**, first came to stay at Tafarn-y-Gelyn
when Enid was convalescing after pneumonia in the late 1940s.* They got on
well with Rene and Glenys from
the outset and spent many holidays
together after that. Enid recalls:
"We became good friends and have
remained close ever since. I loved
going to stay on the farm as I
enjoyed helping with the livestock
and the Smiths had become like
family to me. When my husband
and I retired, we decided to move
to North Wales so that I could be
nearer my close friends and live in
the countryside I like so much."

*Joan and Enid
helping with
haymaking on the
farm*

Courtesy of Enid Butler

Jean Griffiths forged a lasting friendship with Barbara Adams who was billeted with Jean's family during the war. "We've kept in touch for over 60 years. After the war I used to go and stay with Barbara in Liverpool and she used to come and visit us in Llanfair DC. We stayed in touch after we'd both got married and have continued to visit each other and to write."

Staying on

Some of the evacuees chose to stay in North Wales permanently after the war.

Sheila Williams recalls: "We didn't move back to Liverpool as Dad loved the open countryside and we were settled in school or jobs. As a young lad he'd often cycle out from Liverpool and I think it was wonderful for him to end up living out here. We had a happy childhood in Mold, regularly walking to Loggerheads or Pantymwyn, saving our bus fare to buy sweets or pop! I used to enjoy going back to Liverpool to stay with relatives but didn't want to live there. I married a local boy and have lived near Mold ever since. I worked at Colomendy for many years and really enjoyed looking after the Liverpool children who were getting their first taste of the countryside. I still like to take my own grandchildren back to Loggerheads."

Some who originally came on holiday have ended up settling in the area too.

Sandra Pritchard, originally from Wallasey, now lives permanently in Llanarmon-yn-Iâl. "I grew up here, spending almost every weekend and all

The Clwydian Range from the Vale of Clwyd

Courtesy of Carl Rogers

the school holidays at my family's caravan at Parc Farm, Llanarmon, in the 1960s and 70s. I started helping to collect glasses in the bar and, when I left school, I stayed on here working at the site. I am now selling caravans and many sales are to Merseysiders! I love living here – the whole way of life is more relaxed than in the city."

Many others returned to Merseyside but later moved back to live in North East Wales in later life.

Barbara Burrows, *who had been evacuated to Bryn Eglwys, has ended up living nearby. "After the war I used to go back for holidays staying with Dorice, who had lived on the farm next door, and we remained close friends. I lived in Liverpool throughout my married life but, after I was widowed, I met up with Bob Abrahams, who had also been evacuated to a farm in Bryn Eglwys. He really loved the rural life and had moved back to North Wales, working as a milkman in Ruthin. Eventually, I moved back to live near Ruthin with Bob and have enjoyed living there ever since."*

Colin Legg *first came to the area as an evacuee, staying briefly in Cilcain and later at Rhes-y-cae, where his guardians had bought a cottage that he stayed in during the war and later for holidays: "I returned to Liverpool after the war and later taught on the Wirral. However, the Moel Famau area left a lasting impression on me and, when I retired, I moved back to the cottage in Rhes-y-cae.*

Nancy Willan spent many years in Cilcain during the war and for childhood holidays: *"Circumstances later took me to live in Essex, where I spent more than 50 years, but eventually, Hiraeth (longing) for the mountains proved too strong and I came back to the area in 1997."*

Colin Swinscoe was born in Liverpool but, when his sister moved to the Loggerheads area to work as a health visitor in Mold, he used to visit her regularly. When he retired in 1970, he moved to live with her. Now in his 90s, he still lives locally in Denbigh. He recalls: *"I love the Loggerheads area and used to walk for miles with my dog, including through Pothole Valley to the other side of Maeshafn; through Colomendy, over Moel Findeg and onto the Rainbow Inn, and up Moel Famau to picnic at the Jubilee Tower."*

Derek Parsons is now living in Pantymwyn, close to where he spent many childhood holidays. *"I felt at home straightaway and all the paths seemed so familiar."*

Revisiting old haunts

Most of those who came as children have come back for regular holidays or visits. Some have bought caravans in the area and spend much of their retirement over here whereas others just come for the occasional visit.

Mr Alick Stark (seated left) with his family at Nant Alyn

Courtesy of Ian Morris

Alick Stark has been coming to Nant Alyn, Rhydymwyn for over 65 years, since his evacuation to the area and subsequent holidays at the caravan park. "Many years after our first visits to Nant Alyn, my grown-up daughter revisited the caravan site and bought a caravan shortly afterwards. Our family have had two caravans on the site for about 14 years now and 4 generations of our family all love to come and stay - my wife and I, our 2 children, our grandchildren and now a great grandchild too! My wife and I come as often as we can; for us, coming to Nant Alyn is like stepping back in time."

Alan Roach's family had been evacuated to Plas Draw, Llangynhafal. "The major invited us back for holidays and we went every year until he died in 1953. We'd spend the whole of the 6 week holiday there and sometimes cousins and other relatives came as well. As an adult, I've taken my children and my grandchildren back up Moel Famau picking bilberries.

Margaret Whalley had been evacuated to Pontblyddyn, "After the war finished I used to come back for holidays with the Roberts family who had been so kind to me and am still in touch with the childhood friend I made there, Marion Booth. I loved living in Pontblyddyn and, if I hadn't had to return to Liverpool after the war, I would have probably spent the rest of my life around there. In 1966 we bought a caravan near Denbigh because of my happy memories of the surrounding area. It had a big window overlooking Moel Famau, which I really enjoyed."

An appreciation of the countryside and its wildlife

Another lasting legacy for almost all those who visited as youngsters is a deep love of the countryside, whether it be a passion for hill walking or an appreciation of the natural world.

Alan Roach remembers: "I remember watching badgers in the nearby sett and looking carefully at a dead badger that had been shot by a farmer. An older boy from a local farm lifted me up to see birds in a nest – I was amazed at their bright colours and found out from my set of coloured Players bird cigarette cards that they were bullfinches – until then I hadn't realised that the vivid colours were so realistic! I'll always remember the yellowhammer singing on the top of a tree too and there was a rowan tree on the mountain – the only tree – with a raven's nest in it. Once I climbed the tree and sat in the nest! I got really into birds then and this interest has remained with me. As an adult I was a founder member of the Wirral Barn Owl Group."

Bob Griffiths, originally from Tranmere, has retired to North Wales and now spends much of his spare time volunteering with Denbighshire Countryside Service. "My love for the countryside and landscape started with the Scouts and that fascination has stayed with me all my life. Now I am trying to repay those happy, carefree and memorable times by giving my free time to the countryside service. I work alongside other dedicated volunteer friends doing all manner of practical tasks, including dry stone walling, heather regeneration, footpath erosion work, hedge-laying or pond restoration led by Denbighshire Countryside Service staff. I'm enjoying doing my bit to conserve the landscape that has meant so much to me."

Ron Plummer recalls: "My holidays with my Uncle Carl at Lixwm have triggered a life-long interest in wildlife and bird-watching in particular. The Loggerheads area still has a great 'pull' and I now help to monitor the black grouse population on the Clwydian Range."

Bob Griffiths (on left) and other volunteers working on heather regeneration on Moel Famau

Courtesy of Denbighshire Countryside Service

Jackie Robertson, one of the 'caravan crew' who regularly came to stay at Bryn Bowlio, Llanferres wrote: "We owe the valley a great deal, in the life-time of happy memories, the great outdoor knowledge we have of trees, flowers, rocks, birds and insects, and a close knowledge of the Llanferres area."

Another member of the group, **Vic Mason**, reflected: "As well as arousing a life-long interest in the Biological Sciences, my early visits to the caravan and the Moel Famau area inspired a lasting concern for wildlife conservation. We must defend such jewels against unsympathetic development".

The influence of Colomendy

Colomendy has had a huge influence on many of its ex-pupils, particularly those who boarded for long periods. Many attribute their lasting interest in the countryside and love of walking to their Colomendy experiences and have developed strong ties to the area.

Some 'caravan crew' members at the 50th Anniversary of Llanferres Village Hall, 2008

Rita Sharp explains: "I co-founded the Colomendy Connection in 1989 for those who want to share their memories of their time boarding in the wooden camps at Colomendy. Since 1990, we have held annual reunions there and the numbers attending have steadily grown. Colomendy and the countryside around it will always be special to us. We call it a 'Little bit of Liverpool in Wales'."

Joan Lucas spent 2 happy years at Colomendy in the 1960s. "I still go back regularly to walk with the Colomendy Ramblers and really enjoy walking in the countryside I learned to love as a child, re-treading the same familiar footpaths."

John Hughes, who runs Bryn Tirion Bed and Breakfast at Maeshafn comments: "We've had several guests who are taking a trip down 'Memory Lane'. The footpath in front of the house runs down through Colomendy and several ex-pupils have found us by chance whilst exploring their old haunts.

Anne Ashcroft spent 5 years at Colomendy in the 1950s. "Colomendy and the surrounding countryside has had a lasting impact on me. My mother bought a caravan at Coed Mawr, Pantymwyn, and, later, my brother and cousins, who had also been at Colomendy, bought caravans there too, as we were all so fond of the area. I spent many happy holidays there with my own children. We'd often take groups of children from the site on a walk through the woods and across Devil's Gorge to the river at Loggerheads, sharing all the

Ysgol Terrig river-dipping at Loggerheads

Courtesy of Denbighshire Countryside Service

knowledge we'd gained at Colomendy about the swallow holes, lead-mining and wildlife. I also still bring children from the playscheme I run for trips to Loggerheads. It never ceases to work its magic!"

Darryl Gregson, *who boarded at Glan Alyn, Colomendy, for 8 years reflects: "I've travelled the world with my work but think the countryside around Loggerheads and Moel Famau is hard to beat – one of the most beautiful areas I've ever visited. I've come full circle now and am trying to buy a plot of land near Colomendy to build my own house."*

Darryl Gregson in the snow on Moel Famau

Courtesy of Darryl Gregson

Even some of those who just came to Colomendy Environmental Studies Centre for a week or two feel it has had an influence on them into adulthood.

Gordon Davies *visited Colomendy in the 1950s. "I have always been glad I went, as ever since, I have loved the outdoors, and my favourite hobby has been walking the hills and mountains. Moel Famau has been 'conquered' many times since, but whenever I am there, I always think back to my first holiday at Colomendy."*

Gordon Jones, *who stayed at Colomendy several times during his schooldays reflects, "My association with the area continues. Now that the kids have left home I have returned to cycling and one of our regular rides is to Loggerheads. My wife and I still enjoy walking in the Clwydian Hills and I'm sure the appeal of the area will always be there."*

Passing on their love of the countryside

Some of those whose interest in the environment and outdoors was triggered by childhood trips to the North Wales countryside themselves are now bringing youngsters back to the same area to try and kindle the same interest for them. Several of those who first came with the Guides, Scouts or Boys' Brigades later became leaders themselves. Other early visitors later became teachers and have brought educational groups to the area.

Former evacuee **Barbara Adams** *trained as a teacher at Bangor and taught at various Liverpool schools. "During this time I took many groups of children to Colomendy and got great pleasure from introducing them to the countryside I had come to love during my evacuation."*

Allan Shaw *from Wallasey, first became hooked on outdoor pursuits when, as a teenager, he used to get the bus to Loggerheads and spend weekends camping in Devil's Gorge. "This love has stayed with me and I am now an Outdoor Education teacher at Knowsley Community College and a Duke of Edinburgh Award Assessor for Wirral, introducing hundreds of Merseyside teenagers to the outdoor life. I often use the Clwydian Range for Duke of Edinburgh work and for the development of teamwork and leadership as well as teaching rock climbing on some of the limestone cliffs."*

The Liverpool Capital
of Culture Celebration,
August 2008.

Above left: Members
of the Colomendy
Connection with the
Moelfamalambanana

Above right: Batala
performing at the
Jubilee Tower

Bottom left: The
Crosville bus arriving at
Moel Famau car park

Lasting a lifetime

Even those who are no longer able to revisit their old haunts still have strong ties with the area. It seems that this affinity lasts a lifetime.

Pat Gore's family were from Waterloo but she was born in Denbigh, during the war and spent her first 6 years in North Wales. "I have lived in Waterloo or Crosby ever since but still feel I am a country girl at heart".

Kathryn Adams, daughter of former evacuee Barbara, says, "Mum really loves the landscape of the Clwydian Range and has asked us to scatter her ashes on the top of Moel Famau."

Visitors today

Recent visitor surveys at Loggerheads and Moel Famau show that the area has not lost its appeal for Merseysiders. The majority of visitors are still from Merseyside and Cheshire and most are repeat visitors including many who have been coming for decades. Some of the those who first came as children are now returning with their own children and grandchildren and enjoy showing them the paths and places that they had loved so much.

Moelfamalambanana!

The cultural links between the Clwydian Range AONB and Liverpool were celebrated in a very visual way in August 2008 when a superlambanana was placed beside the Jubilee Tower on the summit of Moel Famau as part of Liverpool's European Capital of Culture celebrations in 2008. The Moelfamalambanana, as it became known, was the highest on the popular Superlambanana Trail!

The Clwydian Range spans the border of Flintshire and Denbighshire and officers from both councils worked in partnership to organise the project that ran for several months. The undecorated superlambanana made its first appearance in North Wales at the '08 Llangollen Eisteddford where artist, Mai Thomas, used it as a centre piece to inspire members of the public to make felt that was used to produce a decorative harness and saddle. It was then brought to Wepre Park, where over 100 school children from 4 local schools made more decorations for the saddle and harness with artist, Jenny Lee Hill. The final product was a technicolour felt saddle and amazing woven halter, harness and boots, made of the individual sections of artwork from over 500 local people. The superlambanana was painted purple to represent the heather on Moel Famau, its saddle, harness and boots were attached and it was sealed with yacht varnish to withstand the elements, before being installed on Moel Famau.

On Saturday 16th August, about 700 hundred people joined the Big Walk up Moel Famau to see the official unveiling of the Moelfamalambanana, at a lively musical event that attracted people from both Merseyside and North Wales. An old Crosville bus ferried passengers from Mold to the base of Moel Famau, adding a nostalgic flavour to the day, and many of the visitors had long links with the area, including members of the Colomendy Connection.

During August thousands of extra visitors made the effort to climb Moel Famau before the Superlambanana Trail ended. Cat-sized replica superlambananas are now permanent display at Wepre Park and Loggerheads Country Park as mementos of the role Moel Famau played in Liverpool's European Capital of Culture 08 celebrations.

Jane Davies, originally from Birkenhead but now living in Gwernymynydd, near Loggerheads, sent a message to commemorate the superlambanana event. Loggerheads had been a favourite haunt for Jane's parents, and they brought Jane for regular days out to Loggerheads and Moel Famau when she was a child. Later she met her Welsh husband when he was studying at Liverpool University and subsequently they moved to live in North Wales. Her note encapsulates the spirit of this book, celebrating the strong ties between Merseyside and North Wales and makes a fitting end-note.

Extract from Jane Davies' letter, August 2008

" I am a Merseysider, now living in Mold. As a 3 year old, my mum first carried me up Moel Famau - it seemed like being on top of the world. Now I carry my 3 year old up there - my gorgeous half-Welsh, half-Merseyside little girl. She speaks Welsh and supports Liverpool Football Club. She embodies the spirit of North Wales and Merseyside because she is full of love and laughter. We love Liverpool; we love Wales."

Index of contributors